MONEY SKILL$

FOR YOUNG ADULTS IN A DIGITAL AGE

A Quickstart Guide To Help You
Budget, Save and Build Your Credit Score,
Create Wealth Early, Overcome Debt &
Avoid Common Financial Pitfalls

ROSHEL WAITE

FREE Bonus Content & Gifts

FREE Bonus Gift #1

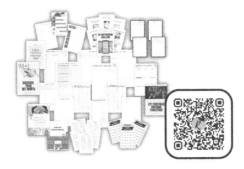

Scan the QR code with your phone for exclusive access to the FREE Resource Library!

FREE Bonus Gift #2

Scan the QR code with your phone to get a PDF copy of the Book for FREE!

To my incredible supporters,

Thank you for believing in me, even when I doubted myself. Your unwavering encouragement, love, and support have been the foundation of my journey. You've celebrated my victories, no matter how small, and lifted me up during my darkest moments. Your faith in my abilities has been my driving force.

To my critics and adversaries,

Thank you for challenging me and pushing me beyond my limits. Your doubts and criticisms have fueled my determination and resilience. You've taught me the invaluable lesson that adversity is not a setback, but a setup for a comeback. Your opposition has sharpened my focus and strengthened my resolve, proving that I can rise above any obstacle.

To everyone who has crossed my path,

You've all contributed to my growth in ways you might not even realize. Whether you offered a kind word or a harsh critique, you've played a part in my story. For that, I am profoundly grateful.

With deepest appreciation and respect. Thank you for being part of my story.

Contents

IMPORTANT - READ THIS FIRST!

Hey there, Friend!

Picture this: a young adult stranded in a flooding apartment. As the water rises, they pray for rescue. They wait, confident that a miraculous solution will arrive. A neighbor knocks, urging them to leave, but they refuse, saying, "I'm waiting for help." Soon, a rescue boat comes, but they wave it away. "God will save me," they insist. Eventually, the water reaches the ceiling, and they're swept away, realizing too late that help came more than once, but they didn't take action.

If this is you, drowning in a sea of student loans, credit card debt, and FOMO-fueled spending. Each swipe of your card pulls you deeper underwater. The very book you're holding now is your life jacket. Are you going to "learn to swim," "or keep drowning." – it's entirely your choice.

This book isn't just about money—it's about freedom, choices, and building the life you dream of. In a world of instant gratification and digital distractions, will you grab this lifeline and learn to navigate the treacherous waters of personal finance?

Your next move could change everything. Dive in, and discover how to not just stay afloat, but ride the waves of financial success in the digital age.

Congratulations on taking this crucial step towards financial literacy. If you're between 18-25 or slightly younger, whether you're in college/ university, working, or starting your career, this book is for you.

Did you know that 58% of Gen Z in the United States (U.S.)

struggle with financial literacy? (The Ipsos poll 2022). And it's not just an American thing – 61% of young adults in the United Kingdom (UK) received zero financial education at school, meaning only 2 out of 5 young adults are financially literate (MyBnk, 2023). You're not alone, and I've been there too.

I'm Roshel Waite, and in my 20s and early 30s, I was drowning in credit card debt and living paycheck to paycheck. That's why I wrote this guide – to give you the financial tools and knowledge I wish I'd had. I've developed money habits that have led me out of financial ruin and on my way to financial stability, and I want to share these life-changing strategies so you can be successful too.

I'm passionate about helping young adults thrive in all aspects of their lives, especially financially. Through my website <https://roshelinarush.com> I share helpful content to help countless young adults level up their productivity and thrive in the school of life.

Welcome to Money Skills for Young Adults in a Digital Age!

A Quickstart Guide To Help You Budget, Save and Build Your Credit Score, Create Wealth Early, Overcome Debt & Avoid Common Financial Pitfalls

In this book, you'll learn how to:

- Create a realistic budget that actually works for you

- Manage debt and understand credit scores

IMPORTANT - READ THIS FIRST!   3

- Make smart investments

- Navigate the unique financial challenges of the digital era, and much more!

What sets this book apart:

- Interactive elements: Worksheets, quizzes, challenges, and more

- App suggestions to help manage your money better

- Immediate Real-life applications and personal anecdotes

- Clear, jargon-free explanations

Plus, there's a treasure trove of other digital extras!

Head to my site, **Roshel in a Rush**:

URL: <https://roshelinarush.com/free-resource-library> Enter your name and email in the form, and I'll send you the password to access all the freebies—whether you bought the book or not.

What to Expect From This Book

Filling The Gap in Financial Education

Unfortunately, many educational systems worldwide do not prioritize teaching financial literacy, leaving young adults to fend for themselves when managing money. This gap can lead to costly mistakes that might take years to recover. By reading this book, you're taking a proactive step to fill that gap and set yourself up for a financially secure future.

How to Use This Book

This book is designed to be read from start to finish, as each chapter builds on the last, covering both simple and complex topics. It provides a comprehensive guide to support you through all stages of your financial journey. For those hungry for more, I've included links to detailed articles on my website.

Key features:

- In-depth coverage of complex topics like money mindset, investing, and debt management

- Shorter chapters on simpler topics, with links to detailed articles on my website for those who want to learn more

- Balanced content suitable for beginners and those with more advanced financial knowledge

The book prioritizes topics that often overwhelm young adults, making it accessible and easy to understand. It aims to provide a well-rounded financial education without becoming overly long or complex.

To get the most out of this book with the action points and activities at the end of each chapter, I recommend using a tablet and a stylist. I use the iPad Pro and Apple pencil, but you can use your computer, laptop, and phone.

Are you ready to take control of your finances and create the life you want?

Let's begin!

CHAPTER 1

The Money Mindset - It's Not Just About Numbers

"What you think, you become. What you feel, you attract. What you imagine, you create."

- Buddha

Let's be honest—when you were a kid, did you ever dream about budgeting or investing? Yeah, me neither. Talking about money was probably as exciting as watching paint dry. But here's the thing: your relationship with money starts much earlier than you might think. Understanding your relationship with money is crucial for financial success. Your money mindset, shaped by your experiences and beliefs, significantly influences your financial decisions and behaviors.

In today's fast-paced world, financial literacy is more crucial than ever for young adults. Yet, according to a survey by the American Psychological Association, 82% of young adults aged 18-25 reported money as a significant source of stress in their lives.

This chapter aims to help you understand and transform your relationship with money, setting the foundation for long-term financial success.

Understanding Money Mindsets

What is Money?:

Money is a tool we use to exchange value. It represents the worth of goods and services, allowing us to trade our work or possessions for things we need or want. Money comes in different forms like cash, digital balances, or investments, and its value can change over time based on economic factors.

What is a Money Mindset?:

Your money mindset is the set of beliefs and attitudes you hold about money. It shapes how you earn, spend, save, and invest.

Why Your Mindset Matters:

Your mindset is often more important than your knowledge when it comes to financial success. According to Morgan Housel, author of "*The Psychology of Money*":

> *"Financial success is not a hard science. It's a soft skill, where your behavior is more important than what you know."*

There are a few factors that can influence your money mindset for the better or worse, let's take a look at the most powerful ones.

Childhood Influences and Money Scripts

Early Experiences Shape Our Relationship with Money

Our early experiences with money often form the basis of our financial attitudes. Family discussions, observations of spending habits, and the general economic environment we grow up in all contribute to our money mindset.

Common Money Scripts

Money scripts are subconscious beliefs about money that guide our financial behaviors as adults. They can be positive or negative.

Common money scripts include:

- **Money avoidance:** Believing money is bad or that you don't deserve it
- **Money worship:** Thinking more money will solve all problems
- **Money status:** Equating net worth with self-worth
- **Money vigilance:** Being frugal and secretive about money

Financial therapist Steven M. Hughes says, *"We start putting together the equation of money and value by age three."* Understanding your money story can help you identify patterns and biases that may hold you back in young adulthood and throughout your life.

The Emotional Side of Money

Money is often tied to our emotions, influencing how we think, feel, and behave, creating money blocks. These money blocks can manifest as fear, anxiety, procrastination, insecurity..., and the list goes on. Ignoring these emotions leads to bad financial decisions. So, take a moment to reflect on your emotional responses to money. What emotions do you experience when it comes to money? Are you anxious, stressed, or excited? How do these emotions influence your financial decisions?

Common Self-Sabotaging Patterns:

This includes overspending, avoiding looking at bank statements (we've all been there!), and chronic procrastination regarding tasks. Maybe you splurge after getting a raise or bonus at work. So many emotional tendencies and money blocks can low-key sabotage our financial goals if we're not careful.

Some common money blocks include:

- Fear of not having enough

- Fear of making a mistake

- Fear of being judged

- Fear of being vulnerable

- Fear of change

The Impact of Mindset on Financial Behavior

Your mindset significantly influences your financial behaviors:

- **Saving**: An abundance mindset encourages saving for future opportunities, while a scarcity mindset might lead to hoarding out of fear.

- **Investing**: Those with an abundance mindset are more likely to invest for growth, while scarcity thinkers might avoid investing altogether.

- **Career**: An abundance mindset can lead to taking calculated risks for career advancement, while a scarcity mindset might keep you stuck in an unfulfilling, soul-crushing job.

- **Entrepreneurship**: Abundance thinkers are more likely to start businesses, seeing potential where others see risk.

Remember, shifting your money mindset is a journey, not a destination.

For example: If you grew up in a household where money was always tight, you may have developed a money script that says, *"I'll never have enough money."* On the other hand, if you came from a family that valued financial security, you may have developed a money script that says, *"I'm capable of managing my finances effectively."*

Identifying your money scripts is the first step in understanding and potentially changing your financial behaviors.

> **Tip**: Reflect on your earliest money memory. How has it influenced your current financial behaviors?

Financial Flashpoints

Financial flashpoints are significant events that shape our relationship with money. These can be positive or negative experiences that leave a lasting impact on our financial mindset.

Examples of financial flashpoints:

- Getting your first job

- Experiencing a significant financial loss

- Inheriting money

- Going through a divorce

Take a moment to reflect on your own financial flashpoints. We all have heated moments from childhood that burn certain money issues into our brains. Maybe it was your parents fighting over bills, getting that first job, or applying for student loans. What triggered a major financial shift in your life? How did you respond? What did you learn from the experience? Pinpointing your defining financial flashpoints can reveal your hidden money scripts.

Financial psychologist Dr. Brad Klontz asserts that managing money has *"gotten tougher in today's society. It's become digits on a screen, and the more abstract it gets, the more vulnerable we are to making mistakes around it."* Klontz suggests we should "make it visual and concrete." One interpretation of this is only to use cold, hard cash that you can hold with your hands and see with your eyes.

Let's play a little game called *"Have you ever heard this saying about money in your childhood?"* By the end of it, count and see how many sayings you've heard. You might be surprised.

Common Sayings About Money

Here are the sayings. Tick the ones that you've heard:

(yes, you can write in the book)

- ☐ Money doesn't grow on trees.

- ☐ Money is the root of all evil

- ☐ Money can't buy you happiness.

- ☐ A penny saved is a penny earned.

- ☐ Money makes the world go round.

- ☐ Time is money.

- ☐ Money talks.

- ☐ Don't put all your eggs in one basket.

I've heard every one of these sayings about money when I was growing up. Some are related to money, and some are related to financial opportunities.

Don't let negative thoughts and self-sabotaging beliefs hold you back. In today's digital world, you can do even better than your parents when it comes to making and managing money. If you are a Millennial or Gen Z, you can succeed and thrive in the digital age. Change your mindset, change your life!

Abundance vs. Scarcity Mindset

Understanding the difference between an abundance mindset and a scarcity mindset is crucial for your financial well-being. Let's dive deeper into these contrasting perspectives:

Abundance Mindset

An abundance mindset is characterized by the belief that there are enough resources and opportunities for everyone.

Scarcity Mindset

A scarcity mindset, on the other hand, is rooted in the belief that there's never enough to go around.

Abundance Mindset	Scarcity Mindset
Focuses on opportunities	Focuses on limitations
Believes in plenty	Believes in lack
Sees money as a tool for growth	Sees money as a source of stress
There's always more than enough	There's never enough
Focuses on gratitude	Focuses on lack
Seeks win-win solutions	Thinks in terms of win-lose
Sees money as a tool for growth	Skeptical of opportunities
Generous with time, money, and knowledge	Tends to hoard resources

Cultivating an abundance mindset can lead to more positive financial outcomes and reduced stress about money.

The Emotional Side of Money

Your relationship with money is deeply personal, shaped by your experiences, emotions, and the beliefs you've picked up along the way. As humans, we're emotional beings. A study by Trampe et al. (2015) found that people experience at least one emotion around 90% of the time, whether positive or negative. In our digital world, our brains are constantly searching for the next dopamine hit, whether it's from social media or spending money on things we like. This can hold us back from achieving our goals, often without us even realizing it.

Money is deeply intertwined with our emotions. Common emotions associated with money include:

- Fear

- Anxiety

- Excitement

- Shame

- Pride

Managing Financial Emotions

1. Practice mindfulness to become aware of your emotional responses to money

2. Keep a money journal to track your spending and the emotions associated with it

3. Seek professional help if money-related emotions are overwhelming

Stories of Young Adults who became successful with the

right mindset

Story 1: Sarah, the Saving Champion

Sarah's lifelong saving habit started in childhood and continued into adulthood. She budgeted carefully, allocating money for essentials, modest spending, and a growing emergency fund. While friends teased her frugality, they secretly admired her financial peace of mind.

Sarah's dedication to saving stemmed from a desire for security and independence, not wealth. Her approach inspired others, like a friend who sought her advice on budgeting and curbing impulse spending.

LESSONS FROM SARAH'S SAVER MINDSET:

Sarah has always been disciplined with her finances. Her story teaches us:

1. Delayed gratification leads to long-term rewards

2. Budgeting enables both fun and financial stability

3. Proactive financial education improves decision-making

> **Key Takeaway:** A Saver Mindset prioritizes long-term goals, financial resilience, and peace of mind through intentional choices.

Story 2: Alex, the Big Spender

Alex is 23 years old and lives for the moment, spending freely on experiences and luxuries. He avoids budgeting, preferring to enjoy life without financial constraints. However, his carefree attitude leads to mounting debts and occasional financial anxiety.

A sudden job loss forces Alex to confront his reckless spending habits. Humbled by the experience, he reluctantly begins educating himself on personal finance, slowly grasping the importance of financial planning.

LESSONS FROM ALEX'S SPENDER MINDSET:

Alex lives for the moment, often neglecting his financial future. His story highlights:

1. Unchecked spending leads to financial strain

2. An emergency fund is crucial for unexpected events

3. Delayed gratification can lead to better long-term opportunities

> **Key Takeaway:** With the right tools and attitude shifts, spenders can find balance between enjoying the present and securing their financial future.

Story 3: Ben, the Amateur Investor

Ben is 21 years old and passionate about the stock market and investing. He prioritizes potential profits over luxury spending, using his earnings to invest rather than for immediate consumption. While enthusiastic about market analysis, Ben initially neglects proper budgeting and risk management.

A significant loss on a tech stock investment serves as a wake-up call, prompting Ben to educate himself on advanced investment strategies, diversification, and risk tolerance.

LESSONS FROM BEN'S INVESTOR MINDSET

Ben's fascination with the stock market teaches us:

1. Enthusiasm for investing needs to be balanced with education

2. Understanding personal risk tolerance is crucial

3. Budgeting supports investment goals

4. Setbacks provide valuable learning experiences

> **Key Takeaway:** The Investor Mindset thrives when enthusiasm is combined with informed strategies, calculated risk-taking, and continuous learning

Story 4: Mia, the Anxious Avoider

Mia is 28 years old and actively avoids dealing with her finances. She ignores bank statements, lacks a budget, and relies on credit cards or parental bailouts for unexpected expenses. Her financial anxiety and shame deepen as peers discuss savings and investments.

A car breakdown forces Mia to confront her financial irresponsibility. She reluctantly begins educating herself on personal finance, starting with small, manageable steps to overcome her avoidance.

LESSONS FROM MIA'S AVOIDER MINDSET

Mia's story of financial avoidance reminds us that:

1. Ignoring finances worsens problems and increases stress

2. Facing financial reality is empowering, even if initially daunting

3. Financial overwhelm is common but can be overcome

4. Small, gradual steps lead to progress

> **Key Takeaway:** The Avoider Mindset stems from fear and uncertainty. Confronting these emotions and taking small actions can transform avoidance into financial control and reduced stress.

Story 5: Liam, the Mindset Shifter

Liam is 22 years old and grew up with a scarcity mindset about money. After discovering the concept of a growth mindset, he decided to change his approach to finances.

Liam challenged his negative self-talk, educated himself on personal finance, and joined supportive communities. Over time, he built an emergency fund, started investing, and developed a side hustle.

LESSONS FROM LIAM'S MINDSET SHIFTER ATTITUDE

Liam's journey of transformation shows us:

1. Awareness of limiting beliefs is the first step to change

2. Reframing negative thoughts impacts financial reality

3. Self-education empowers financial control

4. A supportive community provides motivation and accountability

5. Small, consistent changes lead to significant results

Key Takeaway: Regardless of background, anyone can transform their money mindset and create a more financially secure life through awareness, education, and consistent effort.

Shifting Your Money Mindset to Abundance

Practical steps for changing your relationship with money:

1. **Practice Gratitude**: Start each day by listing three things you're financially grateful for, no matter how small.

2. **Use Positive Affirmations**: Replace negative self-talk with positive affirmations like "Money flows easily into my life" or "I always have more than enough."

3. **Celebrate Others' Successes**: When you hear about someone's financial win, genuinely congratulate them instead of feeling envious.

4. **Focus on Giving**: Paradoxically, giving (whether it's money, time, or knowledge) can make you feel more

abundant.

5. **Reframe Challenges**: Instead of seeing financial setbacks as failures, view them as learning opportunities.

6. **Educate Yourself**: Continuously learn about personal finance and wealth-building strategies to expand your perspective on what's possible.

7. **Surround Yourself with Abundance**: Engage with people, books, and media that promote an abundance mindset.

8. **Practice Mindfulness**: Be present and appreciate what you have right now, rather than always focusing on future wants.

> **Tip:** When faced with a financial decision, ask yourself, "Am I approaching this from a place of abundance or scarcity?

Remember, shifting from a scarcity to an abundance mindset is a journey. Be patient with yourself and celebrate small shifts in your thinking. Over time, this new perspective can dramatically transform your financial life.

"The mind is everything. What you think you become."
- Buddha

By cultivating an abundance mindset, you're not just changing your thoughts – you're opening yourself up to a world of financial possibilities and opportunities.

Financial Awakening

Let me tell you about a book that totally changed how I see money and life. It pulled me away from the usual path of school, 9-5 jobs, and waiting to retire on a government pension. It's called *"Rich Dad Poor Dad: What the Rich Teach Their Kids About Money That the Poor and Middle Class Do Not!"* by Robert Kiyosaki. It's the best-selling personal finance book of all times.

In "Rich Dad Poor Dad," Robert shares his story of growing up with two father figures. One was his biological dad, the "poor dad," who had all the qualifications, a high-paying academic job, and was taking the traditional route to retire with a pension. Despite all this, he lived paycheck to paycheck. The other was his best friend's father, the "rich dad." This guy dropped out of school but built a business empire by making smart investments in assets like stocks and real estate, which put more money in his pocket.

The key difference between these two dads? Their Mindsets. The rich dad had a growth and abundance mindset, while the poor dad did not. It's all about how you think about money and opportunities.

This book shows the stark difference in what rich parents teach their kids about money compared to what the poor and middle class do not. It's not about how smart you are; it's about your behavior with money. You don't need a fancy finance degree or Wall Street experience to become rich. It's about making smart choices and having the right mindset. If you're curious about the psychology behind money, check out *"The Psychology of Money"* by Morgan Housel.

In today's world of Instagram influencers, it's easy to fall into the trap of trying to "keep up with the Joneses." You see people posting about their luxury cars, private jets, and fancy meals, and it's tempting to try and match that lifestyle. But remember, pretending to be rich doesn't make you rich—it's a fast track to debt. Don't end up like Anna Delvey. (If you don't get that reference, watch Netflix's "Inventing Anna.")

Don't let FOMO (fear of missing out) guide your financial choices. Focus on your own goals and values, not what's trending on social media. True financial success isn't about flashy purchases or impressing others.

You've probably heard about lottery winners who go broke fast. That's because their mindset and behavior didn't change even when they got rich. It's a perfect example of how crucial your mindset is when it comes to managing money.

Remember, it's not about how much you make but how you manage what you have. So, start thinking like a rich dad today and watch how your financial future transforms!

Case Study: John, The Lottery Winner Who Went Broke

John Smith, a 35-year-old construction worker, won the lottery in 2010. He won a whopping $10 million jackpot, which he thought would set him up for life. However, just five years later, he was broke and bankrupt due to:

1. Lavish spending on luxury items

2. Unwise investments in get-rich-quick schemes

3. Poor financial management skills

4. A mindset of entitlement and impulsive spending

LESSONS TO LEARN FROM JOHN

Even though John's case study is not real, it should serve as a reminder that:

1. Financial education is crucial, even with sudden wealth

2. Proper budgeting and planning are essential

3. A healthy money mindset is vital for long-term financial stability

4. Overspending and impulsive decisions can lead to financial ruin

> **Key Takeaway:** John's story demonstrates that winning a large sum of money doesn't guarantee financial security. Sound financial knowledge, planning, and a responsible attitude towards money are necessary for maintaining wealth.

This further demonstrates the importance of surrounding yourself with the right kind of people, with the right growth mindset.

"Where large sums of money are concerned, it is advisable to trust nobody." - Agatha Christie

Codie Sanchez, a self-made millionaire and a financial investor in venture capital, recommends reading *Mindset: The New Psychology of Success"* by Carol S. Dweck. She asserts that once you read it, *"you will only want to date, marry, hire, work or hang out with people with growth mindsets.".* According to Dweck (2006), success is dependent on mindset and not abilities and talents.

This further emphasizes the importance of surrounding yourself with the right people. One reason rich people mostly spend time with other rich people is that they have a growth and abundance mindset.

I was browsing YouTube shorts and came across this short titled *"Retired Billionaire's Sugar Daddy Bank Lesson"* (Abundance Wison Channel, 2024), the title made me laugh, so I watched the short, and I was genuinely surprised at how well it summed up the mindset difference between the poor, middle-class, and rich people. So, I wanted to shared it with you:

"Poor people think the primary purpose of money is to pay bills."

"Middle-class people think the primary purpose of money is to pay their bills on time so they can maintain good credit, so they can buy more stuff they can't afford but they can afford the payments."

"Rich people use debt totally."

"Poor people are afraid of debt."

"Middle-class people are used by debt."

"Rich people use debt to create wealth and avoid taxes legally."

"It's a different way of thinking!" – Abundance Wisdom

By understanding and actively working on your money mindset, you can make more informed financial decisions and work towards long-term financial success. Remember, if you're struggling with deep-rooted money beliefs or financial anxiety, don't hesitate to seek professional help. Your financial journey starts with your mindset – let's make it a powerful one!

I encourage you to take the money mindset quiz at the end of this chapter to discover your current money personality. This awareness can help you make better financial decisions.

Action Points

1. Scan the QR code or Click this link to download: **Money Mindset Quiz**
2. Write down your earliest money memory and reflect on its influence
3. Implement a 24-hour waiting period for all non-essential purchases over $50.

GET YOUR MINDSET RIGHT!

CHAPTER 2

Setting Financial Goals - Your Roadmap to Success

"Setting goals is the first step in turning the invisible into the visible."

— Tony Robbins

I magine having the power to turn your wildest financial dreams into reality. Whether it's jetting off to exotic destinations, buying your dream home, or simply sleeping soundly without money worries – it all starts with a plan.

In a world where money seems to slip through our fingers faster than we can earn it, mastering the art of financial goal-setting is your secret weapon. It's not about pinching pennies or living like a hermit; it's about making your money work harder than you do.

Goals provide direction and purpose, giving you a clear target to work towards. Without them, it's easy to lose track of your finances and fall into poor spending habits.

In this chapter, we'll explore the importance of setting financial goals, how to create them, and strategies to achieve them.

The Importance of Financial Goals

Financial goals provide direction and purpose, guiding your financial decisions and helping you prioritize your spending and saving habits. Whether you're saving for a major purchase like buying a car or a home, building an emergency fund, or planning for retirement. Having clear goals is crucial for financial success; with specific goals in mind, it makes it easier to prioritize your spending and saving habits.

Types of Financial Goals

Financial goals can be categorized into short-term, medium-term, and long-term goals. Understanding these categories will help you plan more effectively:

1. **Short-term goals (3-6 months, anything up to 1 year):** Examples include saving for a vacation or building an emergency fund.

2. **Medium-term goals (1-5 years):** These might include saving for a down payment on a house or paying off debts.

3. **Long-term goals (5+ years):** Examples include saving for retirement or funding your children's education.

Setting SMART Financial Goals

SMART is an acronym that stands for Specific, Measurable, Achievable, Relevant, and Time-bound. This framework helps create clear, attainable goals.

Let's break down each element:

- **Specific**: Clearly define what you want to achieve. Instead of saying "I want to save more money," specify how much you want to save and for what purpose. Try, *"I want to save $1,000 for an emergency fund."*

- **Measurable**: You need a way to measure your progress. If your goal is to save $1,000, track how much you're saving each month to ensure you're on target.

- **Achievable**: Ensure your goal is realistic and attainable given your current situation. If you're currently saving $50 per month, setting a goal to save $5,000 in one month might not be achievable. Instead, consider extending your timeline or adjusting the goal amount.

- **Relevant**: Your financial goals should align with your values and long-term plans. If you value experiences and dream of traveling the world, saving for trips might be more relevant than saving for material possessions.

- **Time-bound**: Set a deadline for your goals. This creates a sense of urgency and helps you stay motivated. For example, *"I want to save $1,000 for an emergency fund within the next 12 months."*

Here's an example of a SMART financial goal in action:

> ☒ "I will save $3,000 for a trip to Thailand by setting aside $250 from each paycheck for the next 12 months."

- **S**: This goal is specific, as we know we are saving $3,000 for a trip to Thailand.

- **M**: It's measurable because we know to save $250 from each paycheck.

- **A**: It's achievable, as $250 per month is a realistic amount based on the individual's income and expenses.

- **R**: It's relevant as it aligns with the person's desire to travel to Thailand.

- **T**: It's also time-bound because there is a deadline of 12 months, so we know how long we have to get it done.

Setting SMART financial goals can transform your money mindset into actionable steps. This approach provides a framework for tracking your progress and celebrating your successes. Remember, your goals can evolve as your circumstances change. The key is to stay committed to the process and maintain an abundance and growth mindset.

Creating Your Financial Goals

Start by brainstorming what you want to achieve financially in the short, medium, and long term. Write down all your ideas, then refine them using the SMART criteria. Prioritize your goals based on their importance and urgency.

For example, your list might include:

- Save $1,000 for an emergency fund within 6 months.

- Pay off $4,000 of credit card debt in one year.

- Save $20,000 for a down payment on a car in 3 years.

- Invest $60,000 for retirement over the next 20 years.

> Read the article "**Financial SMART Goals For Young Adults**" to help you set SMART goals, Visit my site: **URL:** https://roshelinarush.com/financial-smart-goals-for-young-adults/

Once you've set your goals, it's time to develop a plan to achieve them. Here are some strategies to consider.

Strategies for Achieving Your Goals

- **Create a budget**: A budget helps you track your income and expenses, making it easier to allocate money towards your goals.

- **Automate your savings**: Set up automatic transfers to your savings or investment accounts to ensure consistent progress.

- **Reduce expenses**: Find areas where you can reduce spending to free up more money for your goals.

- **Increase your income**: Consider side hustles, part-time jobs, or asking for a raise to boost your earnings.

- **Monitor your progress**: Regularly review your goals and adjust your plan as needed to stay on track.

While setting and working towards financial goals is crucial, young adults often face specific challenges that can derail their plans. Being aware of these obstacles and having strategies to overcome them can significantly increase your chances of success.

Overcoming Common Financial Challenges

Here are ten common challenges and their potential solutions:

1 | Challenge: Inconsistent or low income
Solution:

- Develop multiple income streams (e.g., part-time job, freelancing, gig economy work)

- Acquire new skills to increase employability and earning potential

- Negotiate for better pay or seek promotions in your current job

2 | Challenge: High living costs, especially in urban areas

Solution:

- Consider living with roommates to split costs

- Look for more affordable housing options, even if it means a slightly longer commute

- Learn to cook at home and reduce eating out or takeaways

3 | Challenge: Student loan debt

Solution:

- Develop multiple income streams (e.g., part-time job, freelancing, gig economy work)

- Acquire new skills to increase employability and earning potential

4 | Challenge: Lack of financial education

Solution:

- Take free online courses on personal finance

- Read reputable financial blogs and books

- Seek mentorship from financially savvy individuals

5 | Challenge: Peer pressure to spend

Solution:

- Be open with friends about financial goals and limitations

- Suggest low-cost social activities

- Learn to say no to unnecessary expenses without feeling guilty

6 | Challenge: Unexpected expenses

Solution:

- Build an emergency fund (aim for 3-6 months of living

expenses)

- Get appropriate insurance coverage (health, renter's insurance, etc.)

- Learn basic skills to handle minor emergencies (e.g., simple car or home repairs)

7 | Challenge: Difficulty tracking expenses

Solution:

- Use budgeting apps to automatically categorize spending

- Implement a cash envelope system for discretionary spending

- Review bank statements regularly

8 | Challenge: Balancing short-term enjoyment with long-term goals

Solution:

- Allocate a small portion of income for "fun money"

- Find free or low-cost ways to enjoy life

- Focus on experiences rather than material possessions

9 | Challenge: Lifestyle inflation as income increases
Solution:

- Stick to a budget even after pay raises

- Automatically direct additional income to savings or investments

- Regularly reassess and adjust financial goals

10 | Challenge: Lack of motivation or discipline
Solution:

- Set smaller, achievable milestones to build confidence

- Use visual aids (charts, graphs) to track progress

- Find an accountability partner or join a financial support group

Staying Motivated

Achieving financial goals can take time and effort, so it's important to stay motivated. Here are some tips to keep you inspired:

- **Visualize your goals**: Create a vision board or use a goal-tracking app to visualize your progress.

- **Celebrate milestones**: Reward yourself when you reach significant milestones, like paying off a debt or hitting a savings target.

- **Stay flexible**: Life can be unpredictable, so be prepared to adjust your goals and plans as needed.

- **Seek support**: Share your goals with friends or family members who can offer encouragement and accountability.

Remember, if your parents are not rich and you're not expecting to inherit a fortune or at least enough money to set you up for the rest of your life, you may have to fend for yourself!

Setting financial goals is the foundation of successful money management. By defining what you want to achieve and creating a plan to get there, you'll be better equipped to make informed financial decisions and stay on track. Remember, it's never too early or too late to start setting goals and taking control of your financial future.

Action Points

1. Scan the QR code below or Click to Download: **SMART Goal Setting Template**

2. Set three SMART financial goals for yourself (x1 short-term, x1 medium-term and x1 long-term)

3. Write them down & place them where you'll see them daily, like in your bedroom/ bathroom mirror or as a reminder on your phone

---

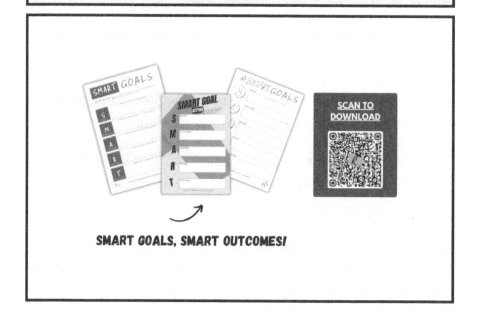

SMART GOALS, SMART OUTCOMES!

CHAPTER 3

Budgeting Basics - Where Does My Money Even Go?

"A budget is telling your money where to go instead of wondering where it went."

- Dave Ramsey

D o you find your money disappearing quickly? One minute, you're doing well, and the next, you're counting pennies. You're not alone. This is why budgeting is essential. Budgeting isn't about saying no to fun, it's about saying yes to your priorities. Budgeting lets you spend guilt-free on stuff you love, knowing your bills are covered, and your goals are getting closer.

As a young adult stepping into the world of financial independence, creating a budget might seem like a daunting task. You might be thinking, "Do I really need this?" The answer is a resounding yes! Budgeting is not just about restricting your spending or being frugal; it's about empowering yourself to make informed financial decisions that align with your goals and values.

Let's explore how tracking your spending can revolutionize your budget, especially in a digital age where both can easily slip through your fingers.

Understanding Your Financial Baseline

Tracking income and expenses

Step 1: Income Tracking: Establishing Your Financial Baseline

The first step in creating an effective budget is understanding your financial baseline - where your money comes from and where it goes. This process might seem tedious, but it's crucial for gaining clarity on your financial situation.

Start by documenting all sources of income:

- Primary job earnings

- Part-time work or side gigs

- Allowances or financial support from family

- Scholarships or grants

- Any passive income streams

Step 2: Realistic Spending Predictions: Knowing Where Your Money Goes

Next, track your expenses. Once you've nailed down your income, it's time to tackle the outgoing part. For at least a month, record every single purchase, no matter how small.

Categorize your expenses: Dig through those bank statements, grab those crumpled receipts, and check your transaction history on your phone's banking app. Start by identifying fixed expenses; these are the stuff that pretty much cost the same each month, like:

- Rent

- Utilities

- Student loan payments

- Phone bill

- Subscriptions

- Minimum debt payments

- Any other non-negotiable expenses

Next, estimate variable expenses, these are the stuff that fluctuates in cost, such as:

- Food (groceries)

- Fuel

- Going out

- Random impulse buys

- Entertainment

- Personal shopping

- Transportation

- Occasional expenses (textbooks, car maintenance)

Remember, the goal isn't to judge your spending habits, but to gather accurate data. By tracking both your income and expenses, you're taking that crucial first step in caring for your finances.

Student-specific income considerations

As a student, your income situation might be unique and potentially more complex than a typical full-time employee. Here are some specific considerations:

1. **Irregular income:** If you work part-time or have seasonal jobs, your income may fluctuate. In this case, budget based on your average monthly income or your lowest expected monthly income to stay on the safe side.

2. **Financial aid:** If you receive scholarships, grants, or loans, factor these into your income. Remember that loans will need to be repaid, so budget accordingly.

3. **Parental support:** If you receive regular financial support from family, include this in your income calculations. Be clear about expectations and any potential changes to this support.

4. **Work-study programs:** If you're part of a work-study program, factor in this income, keeping in mind that it may be limited to a certain number of hours or a maximum amount per semester.

5. **Summer jobs or internships:** If you earn more during summer breaks, consider spreading this income across the entire year in your budget.

6. **Textbook buybacks:** While not a regular income source, money from selling back textbooks can be a helpful boost at the end of each semester.

By understanding your unique income situation and consistently tracking your expenses, you're laying the groundwork for financial success. As you move forward, remember that this process is about progress, not perfection. As you become more aware of your financial baseline, you'll be better equipped to make informed decisions about spending, saving, and working towards your financial goals.

Methods of Tracking Your Spending

Your method of tracking your income and expenses could make the difference between sticking to your budget or going overboard and giving up on it altogether. Here's how to track your spending in a way that makes it stick and fits your lifestyle:

1 | The Old-School Way (Pen and Paper)

If you're into the tactile feel of pen on paper, start with a simple notebook dedicated to your finances. As you go through your bank statements, write down every expense. Yes, it might sound tedious, but it's incredibly effective in making you think about each dollar you spend.

Categorize your expenses as you go—like food, rent, subscriptions, and fun. Try color-coding each category to make it less tedious and more engaging. This isn't just about making your notebook look pretty; it's about visually breaking down your spending patterns. Do you see a lot of orange for dining out? That could be an area where you can cut back.

2 | Digital Budgeting apps and tools for financial tracking

In today's digital age, numerous apps and tools can simplify the tracking process. Here's an overview of some popular budgeting and banking apps:

Mint:

- Pros: Free, automatically syncs with bank accounts, provides a comprehensive financial overview.

- Cons: Ads can be distracting, and categorization sometimes needs manual correction.

- Best for: Those who prefer a hands-off approach to expense tracking.

YNAB (You Need A Budget):

- Pros: Encourages proactive budgeting, offers educational resources, and syncs across devices.

- Cons: Paid subscription, and a steeper learning curve.

- Best for: Those committed to changing their financial habits and willing to invest time in learning the system.

PocketGuard:

- Pros: Helps identify bills you could potentially reduce, simple "In My Pocket" feature shows available spending money.

- Cons: Less detailed than some other apps, limited customization.

- Best for: Those looking to cut costs on recurring bills and who prefer a simpler interface.

Goodbudget:

- Pros: Based on the envelope budgeting system, suitable for couples sharing finances.

- Cons: Free version has limitations, and manual entry required for transactions.

- Best for: Those who like the envelope system but want a digital version.

Personal Capital:

- Pros: Robust investment tracking features and free net worth tracking.

- Cons: More focused on investments than day-to-day budgeting.

- Best for: Those who want to track both their budget and investments in one place.

These apps don't just track your spending; they analyze it, offering detailed reports and helpful graphs that make it easy to see where your money goes each month. They make it easier to maintain consistent records.

3 | The Hybrid Approach (The Best of Both Worlds)

Maybe you're not ready to go fully digital, or perhaps you deal with many cash transactions that aren't automatically logged by an app. The hybrid method might be your best bet. Please keep all your receipts, and make it a habit to sit down once a week to log these expenses on a digital or paper tracker.

Whatever method you choose, consistency is the key to tracking your spending. Make it a regular part of your routine, whether daily logging, a weekly review of receipts and accounts, or a monthly sit-down to analyze trends and adjust your budget. Remember, this isn't about self-restriction or penny-pinching. Tracking your spending is about gaining freedom and control over your finances.

Creating Your First Budget

Creating your first budget can feel overwhelming, but it's a crucial step towards financial empowerment.

Financial tech platform Intuit (Prosperity Index Study, 2023) reported that around 40% of Gen Z and 47% of Millennials in America between 18 and 25 years old are more willing to spend on their passions, hobbies, and non-essential purchases compared to older generations like 32% of Gen X and 20% of baby boomers.

This suggests that young adults would instead use their money to enjoy their life now rather than put it toward saving for their future retirement.

The study highlighted the "soft saving" trend among younger generations, in which they allocate fewer resources for future savings and utilize more funds for current experiences that align with their values and personal growth than to save for an unknown future.

I've provided a free Monthly Budget Tracker spreadsheet at the end of this chapter, which you can download. With this in mind, let's break down this process and explore different methods, tools, and considerations for various income situations to create a budget that resonates with your lifestyle and aspirations.

Different budgeting methods

1. The 50/30/20 Rule:
This popular method, popularized by Senator Elizabeth Warren in her book, *'All Your Worth: The Ultimate Lifetime Money Plan*,' suggests allocating your after-tax income as follows:

- 50% for needs (housing, food, utilities, minimum debt payments)

- 30% for wants (entertainment, dining out, hobbies)

- 20% for savings and debt repayment beyond the minimum

This method is flexible and easy to implement, making it great for beginners. However, in expensive cities or countries, you might need to adjust these percentages, perhaps limiting 'wants' to 10-15% of your after-tax income.

2. Zero-Based Budget:
This method assigns every dollar a specific purpose until you reach zero. It's more detailed and hands-on, perfect for those who like complete control over their finances.

3. The Envelope System:
An old-school strategy that still works! Allocate cash to different

envelopes for various expense categories. When an envelope is empty, spending in that category stops for the month.

Always Remember: The best budgeting method is one you can stick to consistently!

Budgeting, like anything, takes practice. Be kind to yourself. The fact that you're even reading this means you're on the right track. Think of it as the first step towards a life where money supports your dreams instead of holding you back.

Let's Examine Case Studies

Since the 50/30/20 is the most popular budgeting method. Let's examine two case studies that demonstrate the 50/30/20 rule in action and explain how and why it can work for you, too.

Case Study 1: Maya, the Aspiring Entrepreneur

Maya's a college student who just landed a part-time job earning $1,500 a month. She also has a small side hustle selling handmade jewelry. She dreams of turning her jewelry business into a full-time gig after graduation.

Let's look at how Maya can make her dreams of becoming an entrepreneur come true using the 50/30/20 rule.

- **Needs (50%):** Maya has assigned 50% of her paycheck, which is $750, to cover her basic needs, such as rent (she lives in shared accommodation that she likes), cheap groceries, transportation, and her phone plan.

- **Wants (30%):** She has assigned 30% for her wants, which is $450 for eating out with her friends, the occasional new outfit, and materials for her jewelry business (this doubles as an investment!).

- **Savings (20%):** The remaining 20%, which is $300, goes directly into two buckets: an emergency fund and a "future business" fund to help her scale her side hustle.

Why this works for Maya: The 50/30/20 rule helps her balance her current needs and future goals. She can still have some fun while actively saving to make her entrepreneurial dreams a reality.

Success Story – My experience using the 50/30/20 rule

"Using the 50/30/20 rule was a game-changer for me personally. It helped me organize my finances and prioritize what matters to me. It's the first budgeting method I've been able to stick with consistently, which is a massive deal for me because I've tried so many others. Since I started using it, I've actually built up my

savings. You don't need much money; start with what you have."

Case Study 2: Alex, the Travel Junkie

Alex graduated a year ago and works full-time, earning $3,000 a month. He's a total travel junkie, and his big goal is to backpack across Europe for a few months next year.

Let's look at how Alex can organize his finances using the 50/30/20 rule to realize his traveling aspirations.

- **Needs (50%):** Alex has assigned $1,500 to his needs. He lives in a studio apartment, so it's worth it. Alex's needs include his utilities, groceries, and student loan payments.

- **Wants (30%):** He assigned $900 to his wants, which might seem like a lot, but he prioritizes experiences. This includes gym membership, rock climbing with friends, concert tickets, and weekend trips.

- **Savings (20%):** Alex puts $600 straight into his Europe travel fund. Alex knows this means sacrificing a bit now, but it's worth it for his dream adventure.

Why it works for Alex: This plan allows him to live a life he enjoys while aggressively saving towards a big goal. The higher "wants" category makes sense for his current lifestyle.

> **Travel Tip:** Start a separate savings account for your travel fund and set up automatic transfers. Watching your travel fund grow can be a huge motivator!

As long as you allocate at least 20% of every paycheck to building wealth (savings and investing) and continue doing it for a long enough time (maybe the rest of your life), you'll be on stable financial ground.

However, I currently live in the UK, where everything is cheaper compared to other countries like the U.S. So, it would be irresponsible of me to suggest that you spend 30% of your after-tax income on 'wants.' If you're living in an expensive city or country, you'll overspend and end up broke. So, keeping your 'wants' between 10 - 15% would be better.

I would NEVER recommend devoting more of your income to 'wants' than to your debt repayments (if you have any), saving for your emergency fund, or investing for your future. Creating your first budget might feel overwhelming, but it's about laying a path to financial clarity and freedom.

By tracking your income, setting realistic spending expectations, and rigorously testing your budget, you set yourself up for a deeper understanding of your financial habits and greater control over your financial future.

The Key Takeaways for Young Adults

- **It's adaptable:** The 50/30/20 is a guideline, not a prison sentence. You can adjust the categories to fit your priorities. I adjust mine every 3 months thanks to the fantastic strategies I learned by reading *"The 12 Week Year: Get More Done in 12 Weeks than Others Do in 12 Months"* by Brian Moran and Michael Lennington.

  - This book changed my life; it challenged my mindset of thinking annually and instead got me to squeeze 12 months of things into just 12 weeks. This improved my results significantly in all areas of my life. It got me out of wasting time and money, and I'll never go back.

- **Celebrate progress:** Seeing your savings grow towards something you're excited about is super motivating!

- **Be bold and change it up:** If you've got a raise, re-evaluate your budget and bump up that savings percentage. Your life changes, and your budget should, too!

As you implement these strategies, remember that personal finance is personal. What works for one person might not work for another. The key is to find strategies that align with your values and lifestyle, making them sustainable for you in the long term.

Adapting budgets for gig economy and irregular income

If you're part of the gig economy or have irregular income, budgeting can be more challenging but equally important. Here's how to adapt:

1. **Calculate your baseline:** Determine the minimum amount you need each month to cover essential expenses. This becomes your non-negotiable income target.

2. **Use percentages instead of fixed amounts:** Allocate your income by percentages rather than set dollar amounts. This way, your budget adjusts automatically whether you have a high-earning month or a leaner one.

3. **Create a buffer fund:** In high-earning months, set aside

extra money in a buffer fund. This can help smooth out your income during leaner months.

4. **Budget based on your lowest-earning month:** Plan your fixed expenses based on what you earn in your lowest-earning month. This ensures you can always cover the essentials.

5. **Separate business and personal expenses:** If you're self-employed, keep business expenses separate from personal ones. This not only helps with taxes but also gives you a clearer picture of your personal finances from your business finances.

6. **Use the "Profit First" method:** Popularized by Mike Michalowicz, this method suggests immediately setting aside a percentage of each paycheck for profit, taxes, and personal pay before allocating the rest to business expenses. Yes, you must pay taxes on a side hustle if you're earning over a certain amount! It's country specific, so find out the threshold amount for your country.

7. **Review and adjust frequently:** With irregular income, it's crucial to review your budget more frequently - perhaps weekly or bi-weekly instead of monthly.

Pro Tip: Remember to account for irregular income, such as tax refunds, birthday money, or occasional freelance gigs.

Remember, creating a budget is not about restricting yourself, but about gaining control and working towards your financial goals.

As you start this journey, be patient with yourself. It might take a few months to find the right balance, but each step brings you closer to financial clarity and freedom.

As Elizabeth Warren wisely put it, "*A budget is more than just a series of numbers on a page; it is an embodiment of our values.*" Your budget should reflect what matters most to you, helping you allocate your resources in a way that aligns with your goals and aspirations.

Now that you've clearly understood where your money is going, it's time to take the reins. By tracking your finances every month, nurturing them, and finding ways to grow them, you're paving the way to financial independence.

Action Points

1. Track Your Money for a whole week or month & Create a monthly budget that prioritizes needs before wants and Test Your Budget

2. Subscribe to the Weekly Newsletter on Roshel in a Rush website and get access to the Free Resource Library full of printables at: <https://roshelinarush.com/free-resource-library/>

3. Scan the QR Code or Click here to Download the **FREE Monthly Budget Tracker Spreadsheet**

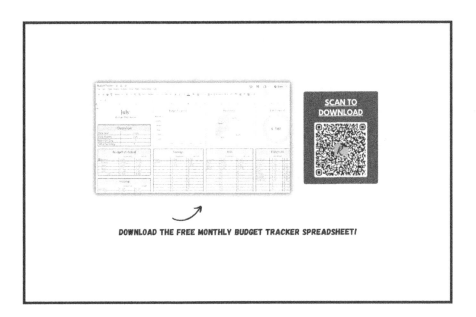

DOWNLOAD THE FREE MONTHLY BUDGET TRACKER SPREADSHEET!

CHAPTER 4

Needs vs. Wants - Making Your Time and Money Work For You

"It's not your salary that makes you rich, it's your spending habits."

- Charles Jaffe

M anaging money in your twenties can feel like a rollercoaster. The trick to staying on track is figuring out the difference between your needs and wants. Let's dive into how you can prioritize your spending to reach your financial goals.

Essential Expenses: Prioritizing Needs Before Wants

First up, let's talk about your "needs." These are non-negotiables that you have to pay for to maintain a basic standard of living:

- Housing (rent or mortgage)

- Food

- Basic utilities

- Transportation (car payment or public transit)

- Insurance

- Healthcare

- Minimum debt repayment

These essentials keep you housed, fed, and healthy so you can work and live relatively stress-free.

Fixed vs. Variable Expenses

Your essential expenses fall into two categories: fixed and variable. Fixed expenses (like rent and loan payments) stay the same every month. Variable expenses (like groceries and utilities) can change. Track your spending for a few months to get an average, and adjust as needed.

Differentiating Needs from Wants

Balancing needs and wants can be tricky. Sure, an avocado toast and a chai latte sound great, but are they essentials? Let's break it down using Maslow's Hierarchy of Needs:

- **Basic Needs**: Food, water, shelter

- **Safety Needs**: Health, financial security

- **Higher Needs**: Social connections, self-esteem, and

personal growth

Remember, the basics now include healthcare, transportation, and internet access, which are crucial in today's world. However, my grandmother and auntie always told me as I was growing up, *'As long as I have a roof over my head and food in my belly, then I'll be fine.'* This instilled a deep need to make sure my basic survival needs were met. The moral of the story is to know your priorities, and never go hungry so that you can pay your internet bill.

Gray Area Needs: Some expenses, like a gym membership, might seem like luxuries but are vital for your well-being. Assess how these costs fit into your overall goals.

Avoiding Societal Pressure: It's easy to confuse wants with needs, especially with social media influencers showing off luxury items. Think critically about whether an expense is necessary or just a societal expectation.

Tracking Time and Money: The Connection

Time is money—literally. It's not just something business moguls say; it's real life. How you spend your time can directly impact your finances, as time can produce money, but money cannot produce more time.

Let's look at some practical ways to manage both effectively.

1 | Tracking Your Time

Do a time audit. For one week, note down everything you do and spend money on, from sleep, work, classes, meals, hanging out with friends, and all forms of entertainment. Including time spent scrolling Instagram and TikTok or other social media that you use. Grab a notebook or use your phone.

A simple spreadsheet or apps like Toggl or ATracker can help automate this with timers and reminders, making it less of a chore—whatever makes the tracking easy and accessible.

This helps you see where your time (and money) goes and identify any time sinks. Don't judge yourself, just be honest!

2 | Identifying Time Sinks

Review your audit at the end of the week and spot any activities that waste time and money. Are you spending hours scrolling through TikTok or binge-watching Netflix shows when you could be using that time to learn a new skill or start a new side hustle? Are you spending hours on activities that drain your wallet, such as gaming or shopping online, or on things that could boost your income, such as tutoring or freelancing?

This insight alone can be a game-changer in adjusting your habits. Set limits on these activities to free up time for more productive pursuits.

3 | Turning Time into Money

Optimize your time by finding ways to earn extra income. Side hustles like tutoring, freelancing, or selling items online can add up. You may be great at graphic design, writing, or gaming. Use these skills to start a side hustle. Platforms like Fiverr, Upwork, or Twitch can help you monetize your skills and hobbies.

Check out this list of 15+ Lucrative Side Hustles for Young Adults and how to get started with them to make some extra cash as soon as possible.

URL: https://roshelinarush.com/side-hustles-for-young-adults/

4 | Investing in Learning

Consider online courses to boost your skills and increase your earning potential. Investing in your education now can pay off big time in the future, making you more marketable in your side hustles or even your primary job.

I use platforms like *YouTube* and *Skillshare* to level up my knowledge. I've spent thousands of British Pounds (£) on online courses to level up my knowledge and generate money-generating ideas that I've turned into a side hustle and a business. Whether you buy a course for $250 or $2,500, it all adds up over time.

5 | Tracking Your Spending

Consistently track your spending using apps or a simple spreadsheet. This habit will help you make smarter financial decisions.

Delayed Gratification

I get it; we want what we want, and we want it now. What's the point in waiting? You only live once, right? For many young adults, delayed gratification is about making informed choices now for greater rewards later and less about having tight restrictions.

It's like the Marshmallow Experiment: those who resisted eating a marshmallow immediately in exchange for more later on did better in life. Applying this concept to finances means resisting the urge to spend impulsively now in favor of more significant future benefits.

Let's explore why waiting is sometimes the best option for financial success.

The Joy of Anticipation: Waiting can make a purchase more satisfying. Save up for things you really want and enjoy the anticipation such as saving up for a concert, a trip, or a luxury item can be more rewarding than impulsive spending.

Tools for Delaying Gratification: Use budgeting apps to set goals and track your progress. These tools have awesome features like savings buckets or automated savings plans which can help reinforce your commitment to long-term financial success.

Mindful Spending

In a world where buying is just a click away, mindful spending is crucial. Make sure your money aligns with your long-term goals and values.

Understanding Mindful Spending: Mindful spending, better known as being 'frugal,' involves being aware of your financial habits and making intentional choices. It's not about cutting all fun but ensuring your purchases bring value and joy.

When purchasing simple, everyday items, I recommend paying with cash instead of your card. This is because these purchases normally slip through your financial cracks. You buy one small thing, then another, and another, but it all adds up. By paying with cash, your brain will associate these things with real, physical money, prompting you to ask yourself whether you really need the items.

More importantly, you will see the cash reducing with your eyes and disappearing in your wallet to less and less as you spend. With a credit card, it might not feel like you're spending real money, leading you to spend more each time you tap your card or phone at the checkout.

The Psychology Behind Purchases: Some triggers lead to wants-based spending. Every spending decision is influenced by needs, wants, emotions, and external pressures. According to Harvard Business Review's study, The New Science of Customer Emotions (2015), research "tapping into customers' fundamental motivations and fulfilling their deep, often unspoken emotional needs can lead to significant business benefits." This is how marketers get consumers like you and me to buy their products and services.

Understanding these influences can help you make more informed decisions. For instance, emotional spending often happens in response to stress, sadness, or even celebration, leading to purchases that feel good but might be regretted later. By recognizing these emotional triggers, you can develop healthier spending habits, like finding alternative ways to cope with emotions that don't involve spending money.

Experiential Spending vs. Material Spending: Research from San Francisco State University found that spending on experiences like travel, concerts, education, often brings longer-lasting happiness, and the participants reported feeling like it was money well spent than spending on material goods (Pchelin & Howell, 2014). This ironically suggests you cannot buy your way to happiness. Consider aligning your discretionary spending with experiences that enrich your life rather than material goods that quickly lose appeal.

5 Practical Steps to Mindful Spending

Step 1: Track Your Spending: Log every expense for a month. Use a budgeting app or a simple spreadsheet to categorize your expenses. This visibility into your spending patterns is the first step toward understanding your financial habits.

Step 2: Question Every Purchase: Before buying, ask if you really need it and if it aligns with your goals. This step can help you avoid unnecessary expenses.

Step 3: Set Spending Goals: Prioritize what's important to you.—whether it's traveling, investing in education, or saving for a future home. Allocate funds in your budget to these goals before anything else. This ensures that your spending aligns with your personal values and long-term aspirations.

Step 4: Create a Waiting Period: Wait 24 hours before making non-essential purchases. The "24-hour rule" is a popular method where you wait 24 hours before completing a purchase. This pause can help you determine if it's a genuine need or a fleeting want.

- **Exceptions to the Rule:** Sometimes, you might face necessary expenses or exceptional deals that don't allow for a 24-hour wait. Use your best judgment to determine when immediate action is necessary. Remember, just because something is at a low price now doesn't mean it won't be reduced again later. Just know that scarcity and time limits are sales tactics that sellers use to get you to buy "now" rather than later or never.

- **When 24 Hours turn into 30 Days:** Consider extending the waiting period to 30 days for larger, more expensive purchases. This time allows you to consider the necessity and value of the item away from the impulse of the initial desire to buy. It's important because these high-ticket items will damage your bank account most if you choose poorly. It's better to play the waiting game than to purchase these impulsively.

For Example

I took out a credit card and bought a new laptop for $1,500 (£1,300) because my old one broke. I could have managed with my iPad, but I rushed the purchase. This led to more unnecessary buys, landing me in credit card debt. The lesson? Think and wait before making big purchases.

Step 5: Track Your "Abandoned Carts": Keep a list of items you decided not to buy. Review this list periodically to validate your decisions and reinforce your ability to delay gratification.

Understanding and managing the balance between needs and wants is essential for achieving financial stability and personal happiness. Adopting strategies like mindful spending, embracing delayed gratification, and applying the "Wait 24 Hours" rule allows you to make deliberate choices that support your financial and personal aspirations. These practices help safeguard your wallet and promote a deeper sense of financial empowerment and satisfaction.

Avoiding Common Money Traps

Frugal people avoid certain common financial pitfall purchases that can drain your bank account. Here are 10 things to avoid buying:

1. Latest Model Smartphone or Technology - If it ain't broke, don't upgrade it. Your old phone works fine, trust me. If you really want a newer version, buy second-hand. Maybe check on eBay or another reseller site or app for a more mindful (cheaper) price.

2. Bottled Water - Use a reusable bottle instead.

3. New Cars - Buy used to avoid depreciation. Used cars are where it's at. I learned this one the hard way!

4. Designer Clothes or Products - You're paying for the brand, not the quality. Don't fall for the "stupidity tax." It's the same stuff, just with a fancy label.

5. Books - Go digital or use the library. Unless you're a hardcore collector who loves the feeling of a physical book in your hands.

6. Brand-Named Foods - Generic tastes just as good. Stop paying for pretty packaging.

7. Warranties and Product Insurances - They're usually not worth it. Take care of your stuff instead.

8. Lottery Tickets or Scratch Cards - You're more likely to get hit by a car than win. Harsh, but true.

9. Cable TV - Streaming services like Disney+ and Netflix are cheaper.

10. Pets - Think hard before committing—they're costly.

Visit my site to read a more in-dept article on these things: **URL: https://roshelinarush.com/things-frugal-people-avoid-buying/**

Remember, being frugal isn't about being cheap - it's about being smart with your money. Start small, review your spending daily, and build a philosophy that aligns with your goals. Your future self will high-five you for it, I promise.

Start small, with a daily review of expenditures, and gradually build a spending philosophy that supports your financial needs and deepest life goals.

Understanding Your Net Worth

Your net worth is a snapshot of your financial health. Calculate it by subtracting your liabilities from your assets.

HOW TO WORK OUT YOUR NET WORTH!

Assets - Debts = Net Worth

- **Assets:** Money in bank accounts, investments, car value, property, valuable items.

- **Liabilities:** Student loans, credit card debt, car loans, unpaid bills.

Even if your net worth is negative now, track it regularly to see your progress. It's like leveling up in a video game—keep playing smart, and you'll hit those high scores.

So, my advice is to embrace the power of knowing your net worth, even if it's not where you want it to be (yet). Remember, your net worth is a number that doesn't define your self-worth or potential. But by staying on top of it and making smart money moves, you'll be amazed at how quickly you can level up and achieve those big financial goals.

Now that you know exactly where your time and money are going, it's time to start planning your financial future.

Action Points

1. Calculate your net worth by doing the '**Discover Your Net Worth**' Worksheet Activity

2. Track your spending for a Week and note down your emotions

3. Scan the QR code or Click to Download: **Weekly Spending Tracker**and the **Discover Your Net Worth Worksheet**

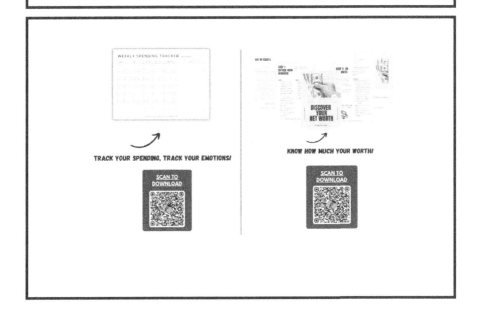

CHAPTER 5

Hidden Costs and Modern Spending Traps

"Don't tell me where your priorities are. Show me where you spend your money, and I'll tell you what they are."

\- James W Frick

I n today's digital age, young adults face unique budgeting challenges, particularly regarding hidden costs and modern spending traps. Let's explore how to identify and manage these sneaky expenses that can quietly drain your wallet.

Subscription services and free trials

The Subscription Trap: Subscriptions are the silent budget killers of our generation. From streaming services and fitness apps to online magazines and gourmet snack boxes, the convenience of subscriptions can lead to out-of-control spending. It starts innocently enough - a subscription here, a membership there -

until one day, you realize your bank account is taking monthly hits from services you barely use.

Managing the Mess:

1. Audit all your subscriptions: List each one, its cost, and how often you use it.

2. Ask yourself, "Do I really need this subscription?" Consider which services you can do without and cancel them.

3. For the ones you keep, check if there are cheaper or bundled options available.

The "Free Trial" Illusion: Free trials can be enticing, promising a risk-free opportunity to try the hottest new app or service. However, these trials often lead to cost traps if you're not careful. Many require a credit card to sign up and automatically convert into paid subscriptions at the end of the trial period if you don't cancel.

Escape Strategy:

1. Always set a reminder a couple of days before the trial period ends.

2. Read the terms and conditions before signing up to understand what you're agreeing to, especially how to cancel.

The True cost of convenience

Convenience has a price tag, and sometimes it's stealthily high. Services that save time, like meal delivery kits, ride-sharing, or quick mobile purchases, can make life easier but at a significant cost. These conveniences can encourage more spending than intended, as the ease of one-click purchasing and auto-fill payment details removes the pain of parting with cash.

For example, **Amazon** has a 1-click purchase option, which makes it so easy and convenient to purchase with just the click of a button. It removes any barriers or extra steps needed to prevent you from deciding to buy the item to you actually buying it.

Conscious Consumption:

1. Reflect on the convenience services you use most and evaluate their impact on your budget.

2. Compare the costs of alternatives that require more effort but save money. For example, cooking at home is cheaper than meal delivery services, and public transportation or cycling can be more cost-effective than ride-sharing.

Alternative Hunting: Become a savvy alternative hunter. Seek out free software alternatives, join online library services instead of subscribing to audiobooks, or use open-source tools for your creative projects. Free or lower-cost options can often serve your needs just as well without the hefty price tag.

Social media influence and peer pressure on spending

In the age of social media, the pressure to keep up with trends and peers can significantly impact your spending habits. The constant stream of curated lifestyles on platforms like Instagram and TikTok can create a sense of FOMO (Fear of Missing Out) and lead to impulsive purchases.

Navigating Social Media Spending Pressure:

1. **Reality Check:** Remember that social media often shows a highlight reel, not real life. That influencer's perfect outfit or latest gadget might be sponsored or a one-time splurge.

2. **Unfollow and Unsubscribe:** If certain accounts consistently make you feel the need to spend, consider unfollowing them. Your mental health and your wallet will thank you.

3. **Wait it Out:** Implement the "30-Day Rule" for non-essential purchases inspired by social media. If you see something you want, wait 30 days before buying it. If you still want it after a month, consider purchasing it. This helps curb impulse spending.

4. **Focus on Your Goals:** When tempted to spend, remind yourself of your financial goals. That trendy item might look great on Instagram, but is it worth delaying your savings goals?

5. **Find Budget-Friendly Alternatives:** If there's a trend you really want to try, look for more affordable ways to participate. Thrift stores, DIY projects, or borrowing from friends can often satisfy the urge without the hefty price tag.

6. **Practice Gratitude:** Regularly remind yourself of what you already have. This can help combat the feeling that you always need something new or something more.

Remember, as Will Rogers wisely said,

"Too many people spend money they earned... to buy

things they don't want... to impress people that they don't like."

Your spending should align with your values and goals, not with the expectations set by social media or peer pressure.

By being aware of these modern spending traps and developing strategies to navigate them, you can maintain control over your finances and make spending decisions that truly align with your priorities and budget. It's about being intentional with your money and making choices that support your financial well-being in the long run.

Hidden Costs in Essentials

Often, what seems like a straightforward expense can have hidden costs attached. For example, that affordable apartment might look great on paper. Still, if it requires you to commute further, you could spend more on transportation, negating any rent savings. Always read the fine print and **consider the total cost of ownership** or usage for the many years you plan on having and using the item, not just the sticker price.

This happened to me when I got my brand-new car on finance back in 2019. I had yet to learn how expensive it would be to own throughout my contract. And that the minute I drove it off the dealership lot, it began losing its value. According to an analysis from iSeeCars.com, the average car loses around 7.8% of its value per year, especially in the first few years of ownership.

Finance expert Ramit Sethi, author of *"I Will Teach You to Be Rich"*, says, *"Car payments are one of the true wealth killers of today that nobody wants to talk about."* and he's right.

As young adults, one of the big-ticket items that you're likely to purchase is a car. So, when shopping around, look for the hidden cost in the fine print. In my car deal, it was the one-time balloon payment at the end of my contract that I had to pay to keep the car. This annoyed me as I had to take out my first bank loan to cover the payment.

Otherwise, I would have lost my car despite spending the last 3 years consistently paying the high monthly payments for it. Fast-forward to 1 year later, and all I managed to pay off was the interest on the loan. If you're looking for a car, getting a used vehicle may be a better fit to avoid those high monthly payments and other expensive, hidden costs. I totally regretted getting a brand-new car at that stage. You should focus on getting an affordable and reliable car that can take you where you want to go without causing you financial problems.

Living Minimally

Embracing a minimalist lifestyle can be particularly appealing and financially beneficial for young adults. As Marie Kondo, the queen of organization, would say, *"Ask yourself, does this spark joy?".* If it does, *"Keep only those things that speak to your heart. Then take the plunge and discard all the rest."*

Living 'minimally' isn't about depriving yourself but focusing your spending on what truly adds value to your life. This might mean opting for a smaller, more affordable living space, choosing a less expensive car that gets you from A to B reliably, or cutting back on subscription services you don't use frequently.

By reducing spending on unnecessary things, you free up money that can be redirected towards savings, travel, investing, or other experiences that enrich your life.

Practical Steps to Prioritize Essential Expenses

1. Create a List: Create a detailed list of your monthly expenses, categorizing them into "needs" and "wants." Be honest during this process—what might feel like a need could be a want.

2. Budget for Essentials First: When you plan your budget, allocate funds to your essential expenses first. This ensures that your most critical needs are covered, and whatever is left can be used for savings and wants.

3. Use Budgeting Tools: Employ budgeting apps or spreadsheets to help you manage your expenses. Tools like YNAB (You Need A Budget), Mint, Google Sheets, and even simple Excel templates can help you visualize your spending patterns and make necessary adjustments.

4. Review and Adjust Regularly: Your needs and income will evolve, so make it a habit to review your budget regularly—ideally, every month. This helps you adjust to changes in income, shifts in living costs, or even better deals on fixed expenses like insurance or utilities.

> *"The art of being wise is the art of knowing what to overlook."*
> *- William James*

By distinguishing essential expenses from discretionary spending, you can build a budget that supports your immediate needs and long-term financial health. This disciplined approach ensures you are covering your bases. It paves the way for financial freedom and stability, allowing you to enjoy your young life without undue financial stress.

Smart Spending

Sustainable and ethical spending

Aligning your spending with your values can lead to more satisfaction and potentially better financial decisions:

1. **Quality over quantity:** Invest in durable, high-quality items that last longer, even if they cost more upfront. This often saves money in the long run and reduces waste.

2. **Support local businesses:** This can strengthen your community's economy and often provides more ethically sourced products.

3. **Research brands:** Look into companies' ethical practices before purchasing. Many apps and websites can help you make informed decisions.

4. **Consider second-hand:** Thrift stores, online marketplaces and reseller apps can be great sources for ethical, budget-friendly finds.

5. **Reduce, reuse, recycle:** This mantra isn't just good for the environment - it's good for your wallet too.

6. **Mindful consumption:** Before buying, ask yourself if you really need the item. This can help reduce impulse purchases and clutter.

Example of Hidden Cost and Spending Traps

I ended up paying for a whole month of Internet Security that I didn't need because I forgot to cancel my free trial. When I called customer service, they said I had to give 30 days' notice to cancel, so I wasn't getting my money back for the current month.

These hidden costs are only hidden because the Service providers count on you being lazy and not bothering to cancel them on time or at all. Don't make the same mistakes; check your spending history to see precisely what you pay for.

Action Points

1. Do a financial audit of your Subscriptions to identify any hidden costs or financial traps linked to your spending.
2. Implement the "wait 30-day rule" for non-essential purchases to stop impulse spending.
3. Scan the QR code or Click to Download: **30 Day Financial Challenge**

CHALLENGE ACCEPTED, WALLET APPROVED!

CHAPTER 6

Credit Scores - The Secret Language of Lending

"If you don't take good care of your credit, then your credit won't take good care of you."

— Tyler Gregory

I t's time to talk about the mysterious and all-powerful credit score. As a young adult, you're no stranger to credit scores. But do you truly understand how they work and why you need to have at least a good score?

Picture this: you're adulting hard by getting ready to rent your first apartment, financing a car, or even applying for your dream job. Suddenly, you're hit with a question that makes your palms sweat and your heart race: "What's your credit score?"

Don't panic! Although your credit score may seem confusing, it's just a tool lenders use to gauge your trustworthiness with borrowed money. Think of it as the secret language of adulting—once you crack the code, a world of financial opportunities opens up.

In this chapter, we'll demystify the credit score and arm you with the tools to build and maintain a score that'll make lenders swoon. So grab a brew, settle in, and get ready to level up your credit game!

How Credit Scores Work

First, What is a credit score? Simply put, it's a three-digit number that lenders use to determine your creditworthiness—aka how likely you are to repay borrowed money on time. Think of your credit score as a report card for your financial habits. The higher your score, the more trustworthy you appear to lenders, and you are more likely to get approved for loans and credit cards with favorable interest rates.

Think of your credit score as a recipe book for your financial life!

The Recipe Book of Your Financial Life

Like a chef combining ingredients to create a delicious dish, credit scoring models combine different pieces of your financial history to whip up your credit score.

Credit bureaus collect all kinds of info about you—like how you pay bills, how much debt you have, etc. They crunch this data into a score predicting how likely you are to repay new loans.

The Five Main Ingredients of Credit

So, what goes into this credit score cookbook? The main ingredients are:

1 | Payment history (35% of your score): Do you pay your bills on time, or are you always fashionably late? Your payment history is the most significant factor. It includes records of payments made on time, late payments, the frequency of late payments, and defaults.

2 | Credit utilization (30%): How much of your available credit are you using? Maxing out those cards is a recipe for a low score. Keeping your utilization low, typically under 30% of your credit limits, is seen favorably.

3 | Length of credit history (15%): How long have you been playing the credit game? The longer, the better. Lenders like to see a long history of responsible credit use. The age of your oldest account, the average age of all your accounts, and the last time each account was used contribute to this factor.

4 | Credit mix (10%): Do you have a diverse credit portfolio, or are you a one-trick pony? This refers to the variety of credit products you have, such as credit cards, installment loans (like student finance loans), finance company accounts, mortgage loans, and other financial products.

5 | New credit (10%): This includes recently opened accounts and hard inquiries in your credit report. Quickly opening many new accounts is a red flag and can signal risk to lenders. How often are you applying for new credit? Too many hard inquiries can negatively affect your score. It gives your potential lenders the impression that you may be in a desperate financial situation and unable to repay any money they may lend you each month reliably.

Different Scoring Models

Now, this is where things become slightly complex. There are other credit scoring models, each with its secret sauce. The most common one is the FICO score, which ranges from 300 to 850. This is the one that the U.S. uses. There's also the VantageScore, which uses a similar range.

Lenders (like banks, credit card companies, and car dealerships) might use different scoring models. So, please don't be surprised if your score changes slightly among them. Some countries like Canada and the UK have credit scoring systems similar to those of the U.S. However, other countries like France and China have different methods of checking creditworthiness.

Unlike our neighbors across the pond, the UK does not have a universal credit rating system. Three credit rating agencies in the UK have credit score ratings from 0 to 999. They are: Experian, TransUnion and Equifax.

1. Experian
2. TransUnion
3. Equifax

However, the five primary factors/ingredients are the same when lenders determine a borrower's general creditworthiness.

The Importance of Your Credit Report

Your credit score is based on the info in your credit report, which is like your financial report card. It's a credit history record, including all your accounts, payments, and any red flags (like collections or bankruptcies).

You can request a free credit report from each major credit reporting agency (Experian, TransUnion, and Equifax) once a year. These are the three Credit Reference Agencies (CRAs). In the UK, you can contact each CRA directly. However, in the U.S., *AnnualCreditReport.com* is the only site authorized by the federal government to issue free annual credit reports from the three CRAs.

We will explore credit reports and mistakes to avoid in more detail later; for now, understand that monitoring your report for errors and potential fraud is crucial to maintaining a healthy credit score.

Building Good Credit From Scratch

Okay, so you're ready to start adulting and building up your credit score. But where do you begin, especially if you have zero credit history? Don't stress—everyone starts somewhere! Here are some credit score hacks that you can use to get started:

Starter Strategies

1. Become an authorized user on someone else's credit card (like a parent or legal guardian). Their good credit habits can rub off on your score.

2. Apply for a secured credit card requiring a cash deposit as collateral. It's like credit with training wheels!

3. Take out a credit-builder loan to help you simultaneously build credit and savings.

4. Open a store credit card (but be careful not to overspend

to get that 10% discount!).

5. Also, there are cards specifically designed to help people build and rebuild their credit scores, so you get one of those cards more quickly than the others.

Proving Responsibility

Once you have some credit accounts in your name, it's time to show lenders that you're a responsible adult. The key to doing this is to pay your bills on time, every time. Set up automatic payments so you never miss a due date.

Also, try to keep your credit utilization low (aim for 30% or less of your credit limit). That means if you have a $1,000 limit, try not to charge more than $300 at a time.

The Power of Time

Here's a secret: one of the best things you can do for your credit score is let it age like a fine wine. The longer you have credit accounts open and in good standing, the better your score will be.

So, if you're tempted to close that old credit card you no longer use, think twice! Keeping it open (and using it occasionally) can boost your score by increasing your average account age.

Monitor Your Progress

Keeping tabs on your progress is important as you build credit. Many credit card companies offer free credit score tracking, or you can use third-party apps like Credit Karma or Mint.

Watching your score climb over time can be super motivating, and it'll help you catch any sudden dips that could signal a problem (like a missed payment or identity theft).

Key Points to Remember:

- If you still need credit, choose one of the starter strategies and take action! Research secured card options, ask a trusted adult about becoming an authorized user or look into credit-builder loans.

- Set up automatic payments on all your credit accounts so you never miss a due date.

- Check your credit score and report regularly (aim for at least once a month). Mark it in your calendar or set a reminder on your phone.

Although having good credit is good news, there are a few things you need to look out for if you want to keep it that way or even improve it.

Credit Mistakes to Avoid

1. Closing Old Accounts: I know it's tempting to Marie Kondo your wallet and close out those dusty old credit cards you never use. But pump the brakes! Closing old accounts can hurt your score by lowering your average account age and reducing your available credit. Instead, keep those accounts open and use them occasionally (like for a small recurring subscription). The credit-scoring gods will reward you!

2. Maxing Out Credit Cards: We've all been there: that shiny new credit card is burning a hole in your pocket, and before you know it, you've maxed it out on impulse buys and late-night pizza deliveries. But here's the thing: high credit utilization is a major red flag to lenders. It makes you look like a risky borrower who might have trouble paying back your debts. Aim to keep your utilization under 30% (or even better, under 10%) to show you can handle credit responsibly. Check out this Interest Rate Calculator to help you estimate various interest rates and decide which is best for you. Visit <https://www.omnicalculator.com/finance/interest-rate>

3. Ignoring Missed Payments: Life happens, and sometimes, we forget to pay a bill on time. It's not the end of the world, but it can seriously damage your credit score (payment history is the most significant factor, remember?). If you miss a payment, don't stick your head in the sand! Contact the lender ASAP to explain the situation and work out a plan to get back on track. The sooner you address it, the less impact it'll have on your score.

4. "Credit Repair" Scams: If you're struggling with bad credit, those ads promising to "fix" your credit overnight might be tempting. But beware! Most of these "credit repair" companies are straight-up scams. The truth is, there's no magic wand to erase negative marks from your credit report instantly. Practicing good credit habits over time is the only way to improve your score. Don't fall for empty promises that could cost you big bucks!

Your Credit Report, Know Your Rights

Your credit report is like your financial fingerprint—unique to you and can significantly impact your life. That's why it's so important to understand your rights when accessing and managing your report.

How to Get Your Free Reports: First, know you're entitled to a free credit report from the three major credit bureaus (Equifax, Experian, and TransUnion) once a year. You can request them at AnnualCreditReport.com, the only official site for free reports, or go directly to each credit bureau and ask them for it. It's best to get one from all the bureaus to see what information each bureau has on your file.

Decoding Your Report: Once you have your reports, it's time to play detective. Please review them carefully for any signs of errors or fraud, like accounts you don't recognize or late payments you know you made on time. If anything looks fishy, highlight it and make notes. You'll need this info to file a dispute.

Disputing Errors: If you find errors in your report, don't panic! You have the right to dispute them and get them corrected. Write a letter to the credit bureau explaining the error and include any supporting documentation (like copies of payment receipts or bank statements). The bureau has 30 days to investigate and respond. If they find the info inaccurate, they must remove it from your report.

Fraud Alerts and Credit Freezes: If you suspect you've been a victim of identity theft, you have some extra tools in your credit protection toolkit. You can place a fraud alert on your report, which requires lenders to verify your identity before opening new accounts in your name.

For even more robust protection, you can freeze your credit report, which prevents anyone from accessing it (including you!). This can be smart if you're not planning to apply for credit anytime soon and want to lock things down.

Check out YouTuber *J. Woodin's* **channel**, where he offers fantastic tips on improving your credit score.

I know we've covered a lot of info! But don't worry—you've totally got this. Remember, your credit score is a powerful tool that can open many doors in your adult life. Practice good credit score behaviors, and you'll be fine. By understanding how it works, building good habits, and staying vigilant about your credit report, you're setting yourself up for financial success.

Action Points

1. Scan the QR code or Click the link to Download the **Credit Score Simulator Checklist**
2. Open a free account with a credit service company that provides your credit score details/ report such as Experian
3. Improve your credit score with the techniques in this chapter
4. Regularly monitor your credit file

LEVEL-UP YOUR CREDIT SCORE!

Be the Hero for Someone Else!

Picture this: you're at a crossroads, juggling dreams, ambitions, and maybe a few doubts. You've just finished an incredible book like Money Skills for Young Adults in a Digital Age that felt like it was written just for you. It's given you guidance and insights that lit up your path.

Now, imagine being the reason someone else gets to feel that same way.

Helping others without expecting anything in return can help you live longer, happier lives, and even make more money. So, let's spread some happiness together!

Would you help someone you've never met, even if you never got credit for it?

Helping others is like holding the door open or pressing the elevator button for someone rushing to catch it. It's a small act, but it means the world. That's exactly what I'm aiming to do with this book – help young adults and budding entrepreneurs like you. But to reach more people, I need a little help from you.

I've got a small favor to ask... Most people judge a book by its cover (and its reviews). So here's my ask on behalf of a struggling young adult you've never met. If this book has resonated with you, if it's given you valuable insights or a fresh perspective, could you take just one minute – yes, just 60 seconds – to leave an honest review?

Why Your Review Matters:

Your review could help one more young adult stop living

paycheck to paycheck, one more budding entrepreneur kickstart their side hustle, one more person land a job that brings them purpose, one more small business owner thrive in your community, one more client change their life for the better, or one more dream a reality.

Please help a young adult by leaving this book an honest review.

Simply scan the QR code or Click the link below to leave your review:

https://www.amazon.com/review/review-your-purchases/?asin= 106874782X

If you feel good about helping a young adult learn more about managing their personal finance, you are my kind of person. Welcome to the club. You're one of us.

I'm much more excited to help you level up your money skills faster than you can imagine. You'll love these strategies I will share in the coming chapters.

Thank you from the bottom of my heart. Your support means the world to me. Now, let's get back to leveling up your money skills.

— Your biggest fan, Roshel Waite

CHAPTER 7

Debt - The Good, the Bad, and the Downright Ugly

"Debt is like any other trap, easy enough to get into, but hard enough to get out of."

- Henry Wheeler Shaw

D ebt - that dreaded d-word. As a young adult, you're probably familiar with credit cards, student loans, car loans, and tempting "buy now, pay later" deals. But not all debt is bad. Some can help build your future, while others can wreck it. Let's dive into the world of debt and learn how to manage it wisely.

This chapter explains the essentials of debt —the good, the bad, and the downright ugly—and provides strategies for managing them, paying them off, and building a stronger financial future. Alright, let's dive into the wild world of debt.

Healthy 'Good' Debt

Yes, there is such a thing as good debt. This is the kind of debt that helps you acquire assets that appreciate in value or increase your earning potential.

Understanding Leverage: Leverage is borrowing money at a reasonable interest rate to invest in something that will generate higher returns over time. Using debt strategically provides some significant advantages. Personal finance means using debt to improve your position, such as through mortgages, student loans, or business loans. Smart leverage is a powerful wealth tool when used responsibly.

Mortgages, The Path to Homeownership: Buying a home is a classic way to build wealth. Mortgages let you buy property, and over time, you build equity. It's better than renting because eventually, you'll own the home outright.

Student Loans, Investing in Your Earning Potential: Student loans can be good if they help you get an education that boosts your earning potential. I know those monthly repayments are a drag but remember Warren Buffett's advice: "*The best investment you can make is in yourself.*"

Business Debt, Fueling Growth: If you're an entrepreneur, a business loan can help you start or expand your venture. Borrowing money to grow a business can be a smart move if managed well.

Good Debt Caveats

For debt to qualify as "good," the interest rates must be reasonable and manageable relative to your income. It would help if you also had a concrete strategy for using the debt productively to generate positive returns rather than letting it spiral into a burden. Good debt only works in your favor if you make it work for you.

It's essential to remember a few key caveats: Always do your research and understand the terms of your loan. Make timely payments and avoid late fees. Keep your debt-to-income ratio in check. Prioritize your financial goals and avoid taking on too much debt. Don't overextend yourself; always consider interest rates, and have a repayment plan in place.

How to use Debt to Generate Income According to Robert Kiyosaki

American Businessman Robert Kiyosaki, author of the *"Rich Dad Poor Dad"* Book, explains how debt used as leverage can generate income. He asserted this goes back to the financial statement which is a combination of two things i.e. an income statement and a balance sheet.

Within this, there are 5 main components:

1. **Income:** Any money coming in

2. **Expenses**: Any money going out through spending

3. **Assets:** Anything that puts money in your pocket

4. **Liabilities:** Anything that takes money out of your pocket

5. **Cash Flow:** Income subtracted by expenses

Debt falls into the liability category to start with. Robert gave the example of a house being a liability and not an asset and expressed that a lot of people are shocked when they hear that.

1. Income
2. Expenses
3. Assets
4. Liabilities
5. Cash flow

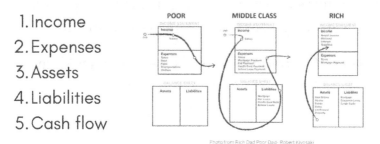

Photo from Rich Dad Poor Dad- Robert Kiyosaki

The poor and middle class rely mainly on their jobs for income and cover their regular expenses after taxes. The difference between them is how much they earn and spend. Typically, they spend what they earn and wait for the next paycheck to repeat the living paycheck-to-paycheck cycle. In contrast, the rich generate income from their assets. They invest in assets that earn money for them.

To understand this, you must first understand the definition of assets and liabilities.

> According to Robert Kiyosaki, (1997), **"anything that puts money into your pocket is an asset and anything that takes money out of your pocket is a liability".**

So, do you think a house is an asset? Ask, does it bring in money or take it out? Think about it.

FOR EXAMPLE:

The average person has a job, where money comes in through income, they pay for their house through the expenses and because the house is a liability, when the money comes in, it goes to a bank through a mortgage. So, it's not an asset because the cash is flowing out.

Continuing on from the house example. If the house was a rental property then it's an asset. The difference lies in how you use it. If you live in the house then it's a liability, even if it's a debt-free house because you still have to pay taxes on it, depreciation and repairs, insurance and other things to upkeep the house.

On the other hand, when the house is a rental property, every month it generates money into your account because you won't be living in it, other people would and they would pay you rent. Even though there would be expenses still going out, like a mortgage you're paying to the bank on the house, once you pay the amount every month, you get to keep what's left. So, you are still making money from that house as the cash flow is putting money in your pocket, which makes the rental property an asset.

Then, you can expand on the investment by buying another rental property and another. Before you know it, you have thousands of rental properties each paying you thousands in cash-flow into your account every month, you can even pay off the mortgage quicker and own the rental property outright, then you'd get to keep even more of the money coming in without paying anything further to the bank. He attributed all of this coming from "good debt" and what makes it good debt is the cash flow.

To sum up: Robert borrows money through liabilities like for a house, a boat etc, turns it into an asset by renting it out and that asset generates money for him through income, therefore using good debt to put money in his pocket. It's all about which direction the cash is flowing to determine if something is an asset or liability. It has nothing to do with the thing you have or want to buy, so nothing to do with the house, the car, or the student loan, only the direction of the cash flow. This is financial literacy at its best and it's something they don't teach us in school, but they really should.

Of course, for any debt to be considered "good", the interest rate needs to be reasonable and the repayment terms need to be realistic for your financial situation. You also need a clear strategy for using the borrowed money productively to acquire an appreciating asset, get an education that boosts your earning power, or start a profitable business. I'll say it again, good debt only works in your favor when you make it work for you.

Final Reminder from Robert Kiyosaki

"You need to focus on assets rather than liabilities. Most people are so busy working for money, trying to pay their bills, and buying liabilities they think are assets."

Just remember which way your cash is flowing. Poor people call it 'debt,' while rich people call it 'leverage.' Ask yourself, which one of these do you want to be? Only you can take action to change your life.

Toxic 'Bad' Debt

Now, let's talk about the dark side of debt. Bad debt can be a financial nightmare. The kind that will slowly bleed your finances dry and keep you trapped in an endless cycle of high interest and money stress. Let's look at a few examples of "bad" debt to avoid.

Exhibit A: Credit card debt.

Credit Card Debt: Carrying a balance on your credit card can lead to high-interest payments that keep growing. It's easy to fall into this trap, so always pay off your balance in full if you can.

Consider "APR" (Annual Percentage Rate), the yearly cost of borrowing money, including fees, expressed as a percentage. Remember the 0% interest rate introductory period doesn't last forever.

Carrying a balance means you're buying things you couldn't afford in the first place. With interest rates ranging from 15% to 30% APR or more, it's easy to get stuck in a cycle of debt. So, stick to only charging what you can afford to pay off in full each month!

According to a survey, 36% of Americans believe paying off their credit card debt will take at least 5 years (Clever Real Estate Survey, 2023). This survey also discovered that more than 3 in 5 Americans (61%) have an average of $5,875 in credit card debt- so if you do, too, you're not alone! Credit card companies regularly target students and young adults with enticing offers, preying on their lack of financial knowledge. This usually leads to massive credit card debt. Many young adults believe buying things on credit is free money, but it's not; you will have to pay that money back with interest if you're not careful.

The Payday Loan Trap, A Short-Term Fix with Devastating Consequences: These are short-term loans with extremely high interest rates, often over 300% APR. That's how a $500 loan can quickly spiral into a $2,000+ nightmare. Avoid these at all costs unless you want to get sucked into a black hole of debt.

"Buy Now, Pay Later" (BNPL), The Rise of Installment Plans: Buy-now-pay-later (BNPL) plans are all the rage with online shopping these days through lenders providers like Klarna. These convenient and slick services let you pay for purchases in interest-free installments, and they are increasingly popular, but they can be a financial trap.

Offering the ability to purchase items immediately and pay in installments is very tempting, but those 0% periods only last for a short while. These plans can be convenient but often come with hidden fees and interest rates that can catch you off guard if you miss a payment. Making BNPL plans are just as slippery as credit cards if you aren't careful.

I avoid BNPL plans and opt to pay with cash or a credit card instead. When it comes to these plans, I now live by the motto, *"If you can't afford to buy the item outright, you can't afford it."* I tell myself this whenever I see an item I want to buy.

Lifestyle Inflation Debt, When Income Increases, So Does Spending: I'm talking about financing a bigger apartment, a brand-new car, and a bunch of expensive new toys the second you score a pay raise - without actually being able to afford that lifestyle long-term. Lifestyle inflation can quickly trap you under a mountain of bills and debt your income can't sustain. As your income increases, it's easy to get caught up in a cycle of spending. Remember, just because you can afford more doesn't mean you should spend more.

Other Toxic Sources: From auto and personal loans to home renovation financing and cash advances on credit cards, tons of other sneaky debt sources can become nightmares if you're not careful. The common thread is the high interest rates, making it an uphill battle to build wealth while clearing those debts.

Downright 'Ugly' Debt

Unfortunately, some debt can have devastating consequences. They are the ugliest, most insidious forms of debt. The kind that doesn't just cause financial ruin but completely destroys your emotional well-being too.

Predatory Lending: This is where debt gets downright ugly and abusive. We're talking about sketchy lenders using deceptive tactics, hidden fees, aggressive collection practices - anything to exploit people's desperation and trap them in endless cycles of debt. This includes payday loans and high-interest auto loans that prey on people in desperate financial situations.

Medical Debt, Unexpected and Crippling: Unexpected medical emergencies can lead to massive debt, even if you have insurance. It's essential to have a solid health insurance plan to protect yourself. Studies have shown that 57.1% of Americans who went bankrupt cited their medical bills as a contributing factor because they didn't have enough health insurance (NCBI, 2019).

Although going into insurance goes beyond the scope of this book, let's take a brief look at the different types of insurance a young adult like you may need to prevent you from entering the ugliest form of debt, depending on your circumstances and lifestyle.

Different Insurance For Young Adults

Here's a summary of the most common types of Insurance you're likely to need to prevent you from slipping into the 'ugly' side of debt:

- **Health Insurance:** Covers medical expenses in case of illness or injury. It's essential for accessing healthcare services, preventive care, and prescription medications.

- **Auto (Car) Insurance:** Legally required if you own and drive a car. It protects against financial losses due to accidents, theft, or damage to your vehicle or others' property.

- **Renter's insurance:** Protects your personal belongings if you rent a home or apartment. It covers losses due to theft, fire, or other perils listed in the policy.

- **Life Insurance:** Provides financial support to beneficiaries in case of death. While it might not seem necessary at a young age, it can be valuable if you have dependents or significant debts.

- **Travel Insurance:** Covers medical emergencies, trip cancellations, lost luggage, and other unexpected events while traveling abroad. It's recommended for frequent travelers or those embarking on long trips.

Additional types of insurance to consider:

- **Disability Insurance:** Replaces a portion of your income if you cannot work due to illness or injury.

- **Pet Insurance:** Covers veterinary expenses for your pet's medical care.

Out-of-control debt doesn't just wreck your finances; it can also take a huge psychological toll. The stress of overwhelming debt can impact overall mental and physical health.

The Mental Toll of Unmanageable Debt:

The constant anxiety, shame, guilt, feelings of hopelessness and despair, and even feelings of being trapped can absolutely demoralize you over time. Debt destroys relationships and erodes your sense of self-worth. Sometimes bankruptcy is the only way to get out from under that crushing mental burden. If your financial situation has become unbearable, there's no shame in seeking a fresh start through bankruptcy.

Bankruptcy

Bankruptcy, When the Burden Becomes Too Great: When your financial burden is so heavy that the only way out is to wipe the slate clean, it's a tricky reset button to hit. For some people struggling under extreme debt loads, bankruptcy is sadly the best or only path to getting a truly fresh start and becoming debt-free. It's an absolute last resort, but filing for bankruptcy can provide the exit ramp from a vicious debt cycle that would otherwise darken your financial future indefinitely.

A fresh start is sometimes necessary, but it comes at a high cost and has long-term consequences. While bankruptcy can sometimes feel like the only way out of an impossible debt situation, it's important to understand the significant and lasting consequences before making this decision.

Immediate Consequences

1. **Emotional and Psychological Impact:** Filing for bankruptcy can be emotionally draining and stressful, often leading to feelings of shame and anxiety. The process is complex and typically requires legal assistance.

2. **Loss of Assets:** You might have to sell assets like your

car, valuables, or even your home to repay creditors, depending on the type of bankruptcy filed.

3. **Limited Access to Credit:** Your credit score will drop significantly, making it hard to get credit cards, loans, or even rent an apartment for several years.

Long-Term Consequences

1. **Rebuilding Creditworthiness:** Bankruptcy stays on your credit report for up to 10 years. Rebuilding your credit score takes time and responsible financial behavior.

2. **Limited Credit Options:** After bankruptcy, getting credit or loans is challenging, and you might have to deal with higher interest rates and fees.

3. **Higher Interest Rates:** Expect significantly higher interest rates on any credit lines you qualify for, as lenders perceive you as a higher risk. This translates into higher costs for everything from car loans to mortgages.

4. **Employment Barriers:** Some employers and landlords check credit reports, and a bankruptcy can limit your opportunities.

5. **Education Consequences:** Bankruptcy can sometimes affect your education opportunities. For example, some professional licenses or certifications may be denied, revoked or suspended.

6. **Public Record:** Bankruptcy filings are public records, potentially leading to social stigma. Bankruptcies remain on your credit report for 7-10 years, depending on the

chapter filed and the country you live in. This public record is accessible to potential lenders, landlords, and even some employers.

Alternatives to Bankruptcy

Before deciding on bankruptcy, consider these alternatives:

1. **Credit Counseling:** Non-profit credit counseling agencies can help you develop a budget and debt management plan.

2. **Debt Consolidation:** Combining multiple debts into a single loan with a lower interest rate can simplify payments.

3. **Debt Settlement:** Negotiating with creditors to reduce debt or settle for less than the original amount.

4. **Financial Education:** Improving your financial literacy can help you manage debt better and avoid future crises.

Bankruptcy is a serious decision with lasting impacts, but it doesn't mean your financial life is over. Explore alternatives, seek professional advice, and remember that with time and responsible financial habits, you can rebuild and regain financial stability.

How to Pay Off Credit Card Debt the Right Way

Here is a step-by-step guide to paying off your credit card debt without paying any interest on the amount you owe:

Step 1: Call Your Credit Card Company or Issuer to

Request a Lower Interest Rate

If you are in financial hardship, call and tell them that. More often than not, they will work with you to reduce your interest rate. This is because they would rather get some money from you than nothing at all. I did this, and my credit card company offered me a 3-month interest rate freeze, allowing me to continue paying 0% interest for 3 months with the option to go on an affordable repayment plan afterward. Either a short-term plan for 3-6 months or a long-term for 12+ months.

Step 2: Apply for a 0% Introductory Promo APR Offer with a $0 Balance Transfer Fee Credit Card Option

With this card, you can move your debt from one credit card to another that offers that 0% interest rate. This allows you to pay off your debt without paying any interest.

To start a balance transfer, you just need to log into your account and request it through your online portal or call the credit card issuer to request it manually. Before you start, you'll need to have the information about the debt you want to move on hand, such as the credit card company or issuer name, amount of debt, and account information.

Golden Rule: Never apply for another credit card with the same company or any other finance company they own where you have your debt. You cannot transfer your debt within the same company from one of their cards to another one of their cards. They won't allow it; it just won't work! Instead, look for different credit card companies to do this.

For example:

If you have your credit card debt with Monzo Bank, you should search outside Monzo Bank for your 0% APR and balance transfer credit card, such as American Express. Just make sure the credit limit is enough to cover your debt. Alternatively, you may need to look into debt consolidation options, which means combining multiple different debts into one account with one issuer and being on one repayment plan.

Step 3: Getting the Correct Credit Card to Do the Balance Transfer

Look for one with:

- **0% APR** - Banks and Credit card companies or issuers offer this as an introductory offer.

- **$0 Balance Transfer Fee** – You don't have to pay a one-time fee to move your debt to your new card; it would be free to move your debt from one card to the other.

- **High Credit Limit** - the amount you're allowed to spend on the new card should be pretty close, if not completely covered, by the amount of the debt you want to move. Some credit card companies or issuers may not allow you to move only part of your debt; sometimes, it's all or nothing.

- **No Annual Fees** - you want to reduce your debt, not add more money to it, which is why you're trying to not pay any interest in the first place, so paying annual fees wouldn't make any sense, especially if you've had your credit card for years. Your bank wants to charge you annual fees based on the amount of debt you owe instead of a fixed annual fee, don't fall for this.

Step 4: Pick Up a Side Hustle or Start an Online Business That Makes Money

You need to earn some extra money, so after you finish your day job, you could try picking up another freelance gig.

If you want to start your own side hustle or online business (more on this later), I recommend you check out YouTuber Brian Jung's channel and content. He's a good finance influencer to follow: **@CREDITBRIAN** on Instagram and **@THEBRIANJUNG** on X (formally Twitter).

Pro Tip: You can continue moving your credit card debt from one credit card to another until you've managed to pay off all your debt. So, before your 0% intro offer ends, you can apply for another balance transfer card, move your debt again, and keep doing it until you're debt-free. It goes without saying, but I will say it anyway: you should never take out any cash at the ATM with a credit card; use your debit card for that.

If you have been unsuccessful with these options, then it's time to explore some repayment strategies that may work for you to tackle and pay off your debt faster and more aggressively.

The Debt Snowball vs. Avalanche: Repayment Strategies

So, let's say you've racked up some debt, and you're ready to slay that beast and become debt-free once and for all. Two commonly prescribed attack methods are the debt "snowball" and the debt "avalanche."

SNOWBALL METHOD: A Favorite Debt Paydown Approach

The debt snowball strategy focuses on paying off your smallest debts first for quick wins, then move to larger ones. This approach lets you score gratifying early victories, even if it's not always the most cost-effective in terms of interest. I'll be honest: this is my favorite method to pay off debts because I can clear off multiple debts more quickly.

AVALANCHE METHOD: The Interest-Saving Approach

With the avalanche approach, you start by first attacking your highest interest rate debt, regardless of balance size. After that, you move on to the second-highest rate of debt and downward from there. This saves you the most money on interest over time. Still, it requires more patience and discipline since you don't get those quick dopamine hits from closing accounts super quickly.

HYBRID APPROACHES: A Mix of Both

Combine both methods by knocking out a couple of small debts first, then pivot to focusing on your highest interest rates once you've built some motivational momentum.

The best repayment strategy is whichever one you can stick to consistently. It's like Goldilocks and the Three Bears; you have to test it to find the one that's just right for you!

The Link Between Money and Mental Health

Debt can seriously mess with your mental health, especially when you're just starting to handle your own finances. Here's the lowdown on how money and mental health are connected:

- **Financial stress can lead to anxiety and depression**: Worrying about bills, debt, or financial goals can cause ongoing stress, potentially leading to anxiety or depression.

- **Mental health issues can affect financial decisions**: Conditions like depression or anxiety can impair judgment, leading to poor financial choices or avoidance of financial responsibilities.

- **Debt and mental health are linked**: Studies show a strong correlation between debt and mental health problems. Debt can lead to feelings of hopelessness and increased stress.

- **Money shame**: Feeling embarrassed or ashamed about your financial situation can lead to isolation and reluctance to seek help.

- **Impact on relationships**: Financial stress can strain relationships, causing conflicts with family, friends, or partners.

Understanding this connection is crucial. As psychologist Daniel Kahneman noted, "*Money doesn't buy you happiness, but lack of money certainly buys you misery.*" Recognizing how financial stress affects your mental health is the first step toward addressing it.

Coping strategies and resources

1. **Practice mindfulness:** Techniques like meditation or deep breathing can help manage stress and anxiety related to finances. Apps like Headspace or Calm can guide you through mindfulness exercises.

2. **Seek professional help:** Don't hesitate to talk to a mental health professional if financial stress is significantly impacting your well-being. Many universities offer free or low-cost counseling services for students. You can even try BetterHelp Online Therapy services, its more affordable than you think.

3. **Financial education:** Improving your financial literacy can boost confidence and reduce stress. Websites like Khan Academy offer free personal finance courses.

4. **Create a plan:** Having a clear financial plan can provide a sense of control. Use budgeting apps or work with a financial advisor to create a realistic plan.

5. **Practice self-compassion:** Be kind to yourself. Remember that many people struggle with finances, especially when starting out. As the saying goes, *"Everybody is fighting a battle you know nothing about."* – so, you're not alone!

6. **Talk about it:** Share your concerns with trusted friends or family. Often, just talking about financial stress can provide

relief and potentially lead to helpful advice or support.

7. **Focus on what you can control:** You may not be able to change your income immediately, but you can control your spending and saving habits.

8. **Use positive affirmations:** Replace negative self-talk about money with positive affirmations. For example, instead of "I'm terrible with money," try **"I'm learning to manage my finances better every day."**

9. **Celebrate small wins:** Acknowledge and celebrate your financial achievements, no matter how small. Paid a bill on time? That's worth celebrating!

10. **Avoid comparing yourself to others:** Remember that social media often shows a highlight reel, not everyday reality. Focus on your own financial journey.

Resources to seek help & assistance:

1. **National Foundation for Credit Counseling (NFCC):** Offers free or low-cost credit counseling.

2. **211.org:** Connects people with local resources, including financial assistance programs.

3. **SAMHSA National Helpline:** Provides 24/7 free and confidential treatment referral and information service for mental health and substance use disorders.

4. **Financial Therapy Association:** Can help you find a professional who specializes in the intersection of financial and mental health.

Remember, it's okay to ask for help. Financial stress is common, especially for young adults, but it doesn't have to define your life. As you work on your finances, also prioritize your mental health. The two are closely linked, and improvements in one area often lead to improvements in the other.

Life After Debt: Building a Freedom Fund

Becoming debt-free is just the beginning. Here's how to keep moving forward:

1. **Celebrate Your Achievement**: Treat yourself to a small reward or throw a "debt-free" party with friends.

2. **Automate Savings**: Set up automated transfers to your savings or investment accounts. Store your savings in a high-yield savings account, such as a Money Market account or Certificates of Deposit (CDs), is the best place. These federally insured savings accounts keep the money relatively liquid but not too available for you to access and spend easily. All the while, you'd still be earning a modest interest on it.

3. **Build an Emergency Fund**: Save enough to cover at least 3-6 months of living expenses.

4. **Set New Financial Goals**: Plan for future dreams like traveling, buying a house, or starting a business. Stash away any bonuses, tax refunds, or unexpected windfalls. Cultivate a money mindset of *"paying yourself first."* We will dive into this concept more in the next chapter. Developing a saving-first mentality will keep you permanently out of the debt trap.

5. **Stay Disciplined**: Continue practicing good financial habits to stay out of debt such as increase your 401(k) contributions or whatever pension plan you have.

Getting out of debt is a big deal, but it's just the first step in a lifelong journey of building wealth and abundance. There will be setbacks and challenges along the way because that's life. But once you've proven to yourself that you have the discipline and perseverance to become debt-free, you'll have the confidence to overcome any future money challenges that come your way.

Keep pushing forward – you've got this! Your debt-free future is looking bright, so grab your shades and keep moving forward. I'm cheering for you!

Action Points

1. Write down the definition of an asset and a liability according to Robert Kiyosaki, and post it somewhere you can see it regularly.

2. Scan the QR Code or Click to Download and complete the **Debt Self-Assessment & Action Plan Workbook**

SCAN TO DOWNLOAD

TAKE ACTION, CONTROL YOUR MONEY!

CHAPTER 8

Pay Yourself First -
The Magic of Saving

"Do not save what is left after spending, but spend what is left after saving."

> - Warren Buffett

L et's face it, managing money isn't exactly the most exciting thing when you're busy with classes, work, socializing, and figuring out life. But ignoring your finances can lead to major stress—just ask your parents!

Here's the good news: small changes can make a big impact on your financial goals. This chapter is all about the magic of saving, reducing money anxiety, and setting yourself up for future wins. #AdultingGoals

You have an advantage in the digital age with tools that previous generations didn't have—so let's use them!

Why "Leftover" Savings Doesn't Work

Forget "leftovers," YOU are the main ingredient. By the end of the month, will you really have leftover cash to save? Probably not. Life happens—rent, food, going out, that new outfit you had to have—and suddenly, your paycheck is gone. If you wait to save, you'll likely end up with nothing left. The solution? Pay yourself first.

Change Your Mindset: Pay Yourself First

Instead of saving what's left, set aside money for savings first. Whether it's $5 or $50, the key is to make saving a habit. Here are some traps to avoid:

- **Paycheck-to-Paycheck Trap**: Living paycheck to paycheck makes saving difficult. Essential expenses take priority, leaving little to save. To break this cycle, treat savings like any other essential expense.

- **Future Willpower Illusion**: Believing you'll save more in the future is risky. If you couldn't save this month, next month won't be any different. Start saving now to build discipline.

- **Psychological Insights:** Behavioral economics teaches us that humans tend to prioritize immediate gratification over long-term benefits, a principle known as present bias. Relying on future willpower to save disregards this ingrained psychological pattern and sets oneself up for repeated disappointment. According to Xiao & Port (Financial Planning Review, 2019), establishing good saving habits now, rather than postponing them, is essential for overcoming this bias.

- **Unexpected Expenses**: Life is unpredictable. Emergencies can wipe out leftover savings. Regular, planned savings build a buffer, helping you handle unexpected costs without stress. Research by the Federal Reserve (2022) shows a shocking percentage (63%) of adult Americans couldn't handle a $400 emergency without going into debt. Emergencies wipe out good intentions every single time. Author Morgan Housel, stated in his book '*The Psychology of Money*', ***"You have to plan on your plan, not going to plan."*** Life throws curveballs, so you can't plan for everything. However, regularly planning your savings protects you from these unpredictable drains.

Strategies to Overcome "Leftover" Savings Pitfalls

To move away from the precarious position of leftover savings, consider these actionable strategies:

1. **Budget with Savings in Mind:** Treat your savings like any other essential expense. Allocate a portion of your income to savings at the beginning of your budgeting process.

2. **Automate Your Savings:** Set up automatic transfers from your checking account to a high-yield savings account. This ensures you save a consistent amount each month without thinking about it.

3. **Adjust Your Lifestyle:** Re-evaluate spending habits. Cut back on dining out, cancel unused subscriptions, or choose cheaper entertainment options.

4. **Increase Your Income:** If cutting expenses isn't enough, consider increasing your income through side jobs, freelancing, or higher-paying job opportunities.

5. **Stay Informed and Flexible:** Continuously monitor and adjust your financial plans. As your financial situation changes, so should your saving strategies.

By understanding the pitfalls of "leftover" savings and implementing structured saving strategies, you can transform your financial health from precarious to prosperous, ensuring that saving becomes an integrated and stress-free part of your financial routine.

Automation Is Your Friend

"Automation is to your time like what compounding interest is to your money." - Rory Vaden.

Consider automation and use tech to your advantage. Willpower is overrated, and good intentions don't pay the bills. Set up automatic transfers from your checking account to a savings account. This ensures you save a consistent amount each month without thinking about it.

Direct Deposit Savings: Set It and Forget It: Set up direct deposit savings so a portion of your paycheck automatically transfers to a savings account every payday. This method ensures consistent savings without effort. You decide how much of your paycheck you want to save—whether it's 5%, 10%, or even more—and then it happens automatically every pay period. This happens before you even see the money, which helps you save more. You can action this in a couple of significant ways such as using:

1. Apps That Automate the Saving Game: Use apps like Qapital, Acorns, and IFTTT (If This Then That), to automate savings. These apps round up purchases or analyze spending to transfer small amounts to savings. Over time, these small amounts add up significantly.

2. Round-Up Apps: Every time you buy a coffee, a concert ticket, or even a new outfit, your change from that purchase is saved. That's what round-up apps do. For example, if your coffee costs $3.50, these apps round up the cost to $4.00 and automatically save the $0.50 difference. I love this; I use this feature a lot, it's built into my Monzo Bank account. Over a year, think about how much that could add up!

3. Automated Transfer Apps: These apps analyze your spending habits and automatically shuffle money from your checking account to your savings account based on the rules you set.

You can adjust settings to be aggressive when saving for a big goal or dial it back when money is tight. I used the IFTTT app for this. I've set multiple rules for mine; one of my rules is transferring money from my current account to my savings account whenever I visit McDonald's. With my location on and a few settings tweaked, the app knows where I've been.

In an attempt to cut down on eating out, for example, if I go to McDonald's, then the app recognizes my location and transfers the amount of money I usually spend on a McDonald's meal (I set this myself in the app) into my savings account.

Just set it and forget it! The less you have to THINK about saving, the better your chances of success.

Types of Savings: Emergency Fund, Goal-Based Savings, Fun Money

Navigating your early twenties can often feel like a financial rollercoaster—exciting, unpredictable, and a bit scary. Setting up the right kinds of savings can give you a safety harness in your financial rollercoaster.

Imagine this: You're at a concert, enjoying your favorite artist or band live, and feeling stress-free because you know your money comes from your "fun" fund—money you set aside specifically for moments like this. Or picture yourself boarding a plane for a month-long trip across Asia, funded entirely by your dedicated travel savings.

Each type of saving serves a distinct purpose:

- Your emergency fund is your financial backup in the "adulting" game—there to catch you if you fall.

- Your goal-based savings are your roadmap to personal milestones and dreams.

- And your fun money? That's your well-earned reward for balancing saving with living.

CHOOSE YOUR CURRENCY!

Let's break down the three critical types of savings that can help you balance necessity, aspirations, and pure fun.

Type 1 | The Emergency Fund: Your Financial Safety Net

An emergency fund provides peace of mind and protection against unexpected expenses. Start small, automate savings, and replenish the fund after use. Knowing you have backup cash is everything. Providing peace of mind is priceless when life gets weird (and it will, trust me).

A study from Bankrate's personal finance website found that only 44% of Americans have enough saved to cover a $1,000 emergency expense. Mark Hamrick, senior economic analyst at Bankrate.com, said, "The partial government shutdown serves as a wake-up call that emergency savings must be made a more serious priority."

Because here's the truth, unexpected expenses will keep popping up in life. The car will need repairs, the roof will spring a leak, and you could get laid off or furloughed. Without a hefty savings safety net, it's too easy to slide back into a debt cycle by charging these budget-busters. An emergency fund is your insurance policy against future debt.

Building an emergency fund

Here's how to build one:

1. Set a goal: Aim for 3-6 months of living expenses. Start small if you need to - even $500 can make a difference in an emergency. It sounds enormous, but this initial target isn't meant to cover everything; it's enough to handle minor emergencies without reaching for a credit card.

Calculate how much you spend monthly on essentials like rent, food, utilities, and transportation, and use this as your guide. Having that emergency fund that you can dip into during unexpected moments means you're less likely to panic. This buffer will allow you to navigate life's ups and downs without financial panic.

2. Automate your savings: Set up automatic transfers from your checking to your savings account each payday. Put the money into a high-yield savings account like American Express, Ally, Marcus, or SoFi to earn more interest (up to x10 times more) than you would otherwise get at a traditional brick-and-mortar bank, or with it just sitting in a regular bank account earning little to no interest at all.

Remember, that money could sit in that account for many months or years. Don't rush the process of choosing an excellent high-interest bank account to stash your savings till that rainy day because when it does, you might find that you have way more than expected because of how you built up your emergency fund and how you chose to store it.

3. Use windfalls wisely: Put tax refunds, birthday money, or other unexpected income directly into your emergency fund.

4. Keep it accessible but separate: Use a high-yield savings account that's easy to access in emergencies, but not so easy that you're tempted to dip into it for non-emergencies.

5. Replenish after use: If you need to use your emergency fund, make replenishing it a priority once the crisis has passed.

Once that emergency fund is built up, you're free to save for the fun stuff and set some awesome new money goals for yourself! With debt off your back, you've freed up cash toward your biggest dreams.

Type 2 | Goal-Based Savings: Dream It, Achieve It

Whether it's backpacking across Europe, snagging the latest tech gadget, or saving for a significant life event like a wedding, having specific goals can transform the abstract concept of saving into something tangible and exciting.

Breaking It Down: Set clear, concrete goals and break them down into manageable steps. If your dream trip costs $3,000, determine how much you must save each month to make it happen. Use apps that track your progress and motivate you by showing how each saved dollar brings you closer to your goal.

Type 3 | The Guilt-Free "Fun" Money Jar: Essential for Mental Health

Allocate funds for "fun money" to prevent burnout. Set a

budget for leisure activities to enjoy guilt-free spending without compromising other financial goals.

Young Adult Real Talk

- **"Separate" Doesn't Always Mean Separate Accounts:** Create multiple 'pots' for different savings goals. Online banks often let you create sub-savings accounts, too. My Monzo bank lets me have one main account but creates multiple 'pots' under that one account that I can put money in for different things, such as one pot for saving for a holiday fund, one for car purchase fund, etc.

- **Adapt to Changes:** Adjust savings goals as your income or life situation changes.

- **Celebrating Wins:** Reward yourself for hitting mini-goals to stay motivated.

Remember, your savings strategy will evolve as your life does. The important part is starting the habit now, so you're in control of your money, not the other way around.

The Power of Compound Interest (Time is Your Money-Making Machine)

"Compound interest is the eighth wonder of the world. He who understands it earns it...he who doesn't...pays it." - Albert Einstein.

Simple Explanation: Compound Interest Unpacked

Compound interest means earning interest on both your initial money and the interest it has already earned. It's like planting a tree that grows into a forest over time.

Starting Early Advantage: The Power of Time

Here's why starting early makes such a big difference. Let's say two friends, Alex and Sam, decide to save. Alex started saving at 20 years old, setting aside $100 a month in an account that earns compound interest at an annual rate of 5%. Sam starts saving when they're 30. By the time Alex and Sam reached 40, Alex had saved significantly more, even though they had only put in money for ten additional years.

This is because Alex's savings had more time to earn interest, and then that interest earned more interest, and so on—showing how starting early isn't just good; it's potentially game-changing. The earlier you start, the longer your money has to multiply. It's the ultimate 'set it and forget it' strategy.

Interest Rate Matters: Shopping for the Best Rates

Not all savings accounts are created equal. The rate at which your savings grow depends heavily on the interest rate. Higher rates mean more money. It's worth shopping around for reasonable rates, especially when considering savings accounts, certificates of deposit (CDs), or bonds, even when it comes to inflation.

Online banks often offer higher rates than traditional brick-and-mortar banks because they have lower overhead costs. Keep an eye on these rates, and don't hesitate to move your money if you find a better rate elsewhere. Always read the fine print to avoid fees or penalties that could eat into your interest earnings.

Visual Tools: Seeing Is Believing: Use online compound interest calculators to visualize how your savings can grow over time. This makes the concept more tangible and motivating.

Compound interest might be the most powerful tool in your financial toolkit. It's not just about saving money; it's about making your money work for you over time. Starting as early as possible, even with small amounts, and ensuring you get the best interest rate can significantly impact your financial health. Use visual tools to keep track of your progress and adjust your savings strategy as needed.

With a good understanding of compound interest, you're not just saving money—you're setting up a foundation for wealth that can last a lifetime.

Saving isn't just about putting money away. It's about making smart choices now that will set you up for financial success in the future. By paying yourself first, automating your savings, understanding the power of compound interest, and learning to save for different purposes, you can turn saving into a rewarding part of your financial routine. It's never too late to start. If you invest $6,000 a year, from when you were 25 years old till you're 65 years old, with the market returning about 10% a year, you'll end up with about $2.7 million.

On the other hand, if you choose not to invest it in the stock market and just keep your money in the bank, then within that same time frame, you'd end up with just $240K. As you can see, the difference is enormous and can be life-changing.

Remember, as Robert Kiyosaki rightly said, *"It's not how much*

*money you make, but how much money you keep, how hard
it works for you, and how many generations you keep it for."*

Make Saving a Habit: Cultivating Your Financial Garden

Turning saving into a habit might sound as fun as eating your veggies, but think about it like leveling up in a game where the prize is your financial freedom. You're building your financial fortress or cultivating a savings garden—whichever metaphor fits, the key is consistency. Here's how to make saving a regular part of your life without feeling like a chore.

Small Wins = Big Motivation

Set small, achievable targets along the way to your bigger financial goals. It could be saving $50 from your weekly budget or reaching the first $500 in your emergency fund.

Inspiration is Everywhere

You're not in this alone. A whole community is dedicated to saving and managing money smartly. Dive into financial blogs, follow hashtags like #SavingsGoals on Instagram or TikTok, and join Facebook groups focused on personal finance for young adults. This one is my favorite; it's called **@theorganizemoney**.

Make it a Game

Who says saving money has to be dull? Turn it into a game. Set challenges for yourself each month, such as keeping a certain amount or cutting back on specific expenses.

Saving isn't just about putting money away; it's about making smart choices now to set yourself up for financial success in the future. Start small, keep it fun, and watch your financial garden flourish!

Action Points

1. Complete the 1,000 in 90 Days Savings Challenge to create an Emergency Fund.

2. Automate Your Savings with scheduled transfers.

3. Set Specific Saving Goals.

4. Increase Your Income.

5. Leverage Compound Interest: Check out this Investment Calculator to see how much you can invest now and what the compound interest could be. <https://www.omnicalculator.com/finance/investment>

6. Scan the QR code or Click the link to download the **Saving Challenge Tracker**

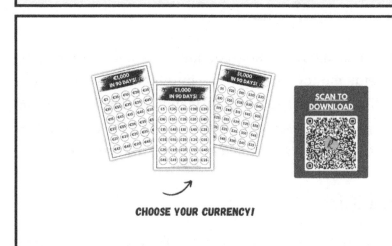

CHOOSE YOUR CURRENCY!

CHAPTER 9

Secure Banking - Protect Your Money in the Digital Age

"Check yourself before you wreck yourself."

\- Meg Cabot

E very bank has an app these days, and as a young adult, I bet you prefer the convenience of using the app to do your online banking rather than wasting your time visiting one of their local branches and waiting in a long queue. But, with online banking so popular in the digital age, you might be wondering just how good your bank is at protecting your hard-earned money.

Let's take a look at some important things you need to consider to help secure your money.

Picking the Right Bank: Picking a bank is about more than just reasonable interest rates, lovely branches, or who has the coolest app; it's about how well they protect your digital information. Cybersecurity should be a crucial part of your decision because a bank's security features can be the difference between keeping your money safe or losing it to hackers.

Please do your homework and make sure they're legit about cybersecurity. Check out their track record in handling data breaches. How good are they at being open and transparent? Look for banks that are transparent about their security and proactive in updating it and educating their customers. Banks that have handled past breaches well are often the safest bets because they've proven they can protect their clients.

Example Of A Data Breach:

> On July 29, 2019, Capital One revealed that a hacker had accessed personal information from people who have Capital One credit cards or had applied for one. The breach affected around 100 million people in the U.S. and 6 million in Canada. Thankfully, over 99% of Social Security numbers, credit card account numbers, and log-in credentials were not compromised. The stolen data included names, phone numbers, email addresses, birthdays, self-reported income, credit scores, and transaction data. Capital One promised to notify those affected and provide free credit monitoring and identity protection. The hacker had already been arrested by the FBI by the time the breach was announced.

This example demonstrated that nowhere is 100% secure, but there are things that you can do to help keep your money as safe as possible.

Double Up on Security: Two-factor authentication (2FA) is a must-have. That's where you must confirm logging in with a code on your phone. It's super annoying, but better safe than sorry. It adds an extra layer of security, making it harder for thieves to access your account.

Along with 2FA, creating strong, unique passwords for your banking accounts is crucial. Make your passwords strong – super complicated and different for each account. With passwords, I recommend using three totally random words, separated by a dash between them. For example: "shopping-money-beach". To make it even more secure, add capital letters, numbers, and symbols to it.

For example: "Shopping-Money-Beach24!" It is much harder for people, especially hackers, to guess your password when it's made up of random words that have nothing to do with each other, even if they are using high-level tech and coding to try and crack it.

Always, check your bank statements and transaction history carefully! Are there any weird charges or things you didn't buy? If so, please report it to your bank immediately! Check out this article on How to Read a Bank Statement so you know what to look out for.

URL: https://roshelinarush.com/how-to-read-a-bank-statement/

You can set up a spending alert limit or turn on the feature on your banking app where every time you spend money, you will get a notification letting you know how much and where it was spent. This is an added level of awareness to ensure you recognize the transactions being made, and it's a great way to spot potential fraud activity in your account.

If you notice someone else actively using your card, you can freeze your card from the app to prevent further spending. It's often a standard feature in banking apps these days.

Keep an Eye on Your Money: Regularly checking your bank statements can help you catch any unusual activity early. If something looks off, you can deal with it quickly, preventing potential headaches. I set mine to alert me of every purchase on my card regardless of the amount spent.

Safe Online Banking and Surfing: Avoid using public Wi-Fi for banking since it's not secure. Stick to private, secured networks or use a Virtual Private Network (VPN), which encrypts your data, making it much harder for anyone to steal your information.

Don't Get Scammed: Protect Your Personal Info and Your Hard-Earned Cash

Scams are a serious risk in the digital age, and young adults are often targets. If something seems too good to be true, guess what? It probably is. Whether it's:

- *Phishing emails pretending to be from your bank? Fraud.*

- *Job offers that ask you to pay money upfront? Fake.*

- *Super-hot celebrity DMing you out of nowhere? Yeah, no.*

- *Investment opportunities promising huge insane returns for little risk? SCAM.*

If it feels off, trust your gut. Scams are everywhere, especially on the internet. And if you do fall for something, don't be afraid or ashamed to report it! It helps stop other people from being scammed, too.

Spot the Scams

Always be skeptical about unsolicited requests for your personal info. Look for signs like odd email addresses or links that don't seem quite right. Urgency is a common tactic scammers use to rush you into making bad decisions.

Scammers do not age discriminate; according to research by Canada Life (2023), 18% of young adults in the UK aged 18 to 34 who had experienced a scam attempt say they fell for the fraud. Email, texts, and cold calling are the preferred methods to target this age group. However, social media platforms are becoming increasingly popular, especially with the rise of Artificial intelligence (A.I.).

> TRUST ME, YOUR PERSONAL INFO IS GOLD!

Scammers and fraudsters are always looking to get your personal info through emails, texts, and fake websites, tricking you into sharing sensitive data. Just imagine the damage they can do to you with it if you fall for one of their scams. Even legitimate companies want your personal info to sell your data to more prominent companies, who then call you and try to sell you things like telemarketers.

Picture this: You're sitting down eating your lunch, and then you get a call from a number you don't recognize. Sometimes, it says 'Potential Fraud' on the caller's I.D., but sometimes, I just say 'unknown.' Either way, you are curious, so you answer the call, only to be asked by the caller if you've been in an accident recently and want to claim compensation or if you want to upgrade your current mobile phone plan to the latest phone but on a cheaper deal.

How annoying is that? Especially when you get them frequently, you're left wondering how these people got your contact details. Well, now you know: one or more of the companies you're associated with has sold your data to another company because you haven't applied the proper privacy settings to your account.

By readily accepting their terms & conditions cookies on their websites, without even glancing at their disclaimer policy and how they plan on using the data collected from you, you've granted them permission to do this. We've all been there; when you first visit a new website, the first thing that pops up is its cookie disclaimer. It's easy to click "accept all cookies" without thinking about it. It may seem harmless, but that doesn't mean it will always be that way.

When you get a call from one of these telemarketers, tell them you are not interested in whatever it is they are trying to sell you and to remove all your personal data from their system immediately. Be polite about it, but be firm.

Okay, before we get into the nitty gritty of common scams that young adults have to constantly fend off, let's look at some other ways you can get your data removed from these companies' databases and systems.

Ways to get your data removed

Here is how you can regain control of your online data – let's think of it like cleaning up your digital footprint:

1. Check the company's privacy policy: Most companies have a privacy policy on their website that explains how they handle your data. Read it and see if they mention data removal or opting out. Look for sections titled "Data Deletion," "Right to be Forgotten," or something similar. These sections should tell you the exact process to request deletion (often an email, web form, or phone number).

2. Direct Requests: If you can't find the info you need in the privacy policy, don't hesitate to contact the company. Slide into their DMs, send them an email, or give their customer support department a call. Let them know you want your personal data removed and ask about the process. Be specific, don't just say, "delete my data." Be clear about what you want deleted (name, contact info, purchase history, etc.).

3. Look for an opt-out or unsubscribe option: Some companies make it easy to opt out of data collection or unsubscribe from their services. Look for these options in your account settings or at the bottom of emails they send you.

4. Use your legal rights: You might have some legal backing depending on where you live, so you need to find out if these laws apply. In the E.U., there's the General Data Protection Regulation (GDPR), and in California, there's the California Consumer Privacy Act (CCPA). These laws allow you to request data deletion, so don't be afraid to use them if needed.

5. Consider using a privacy service: There are some excellent services out there, like Mine <https://www.saymine.com/> and DeleteMe <https://joindeleteme.com/>, that can help you find companies that hold your data and automate the deletion request process. They do the heavy lifting for you, which can be a big time-saver. Some have free basic features, while others are paid services.

Remember, it's your data, and you have the right to control it. Don't be shy about standing up for your privacy. If a company gives you a hard time or refuses to remove your data, you can always file a complaint with your local data protection authority. Depending on what country you live in, they've got your back!

Key Points to remember

- **Only some things can be deleted:** Some companies must keep specific data for legal or accounting reasons.

- **Proof of identity:** Be prepared to prove your identity by providing I.D. or other information.

- **Persistence:** It may take some time and follow-ups. Don't get discouraged if your first request isn't immediately honored.

- **Minimize data sharing upfront:** Be selective about what data you share with companies in the first place.

- **Regular data audits:** Periodically check which companies have your data and request deletion if you no longer need their service.

Common Scams to Be Aware Of

There are so many scams out there that we all need to be aware of. Scammers try to scam you through things you are already susceptible to, such as your hobbies and interests. It makes it easier for you to fall for their con.

Now, let's look at a breakdown of phishing, vishing, and smishing scams that people and companies use to get your data, that young adults should be especially aware of, plus tips on how to stay safe:

Phishing

- **Fake Job Offers:** Scammers pose as recruiters, offering tempting work-from-home opportunities that require you to share personal info or pay upfront fees.

- **'Subscription Renewal' Scams:** Emails claiming your Netflix (or other popular service) subscription is expiring – clicking the link leads to a fake login page to steal your account info.

- **Fake Contests and Giveaways:** "You've won!" emails or social media posts require clicking a link and providing info to claim your prize.

Vishing

- **Fake Bank Alerts:** An automated call claims suspicious activity on your account, designed to scare you into giving up your card number or PIN over the phone.

- **Impersonating Tech Support:** Callers pretend to be from Microsoft or Apple, claiming your computer has a virus. If you provide remote access, they'll install malware.

- **"Can you hear me?" Scams:** Callers try to get you to say "yes" and record it, then use that as confirmation for fraudulent charges.

- **Artificial intelligence (A.I.) generated scams:** Imitate voices, create compelling, deep fake videos, and use public people's likenesses to falsely portray endorsing schemes to manipulate you to hand over money.

Smishing

- **Fake Package Delivery Notices:** Texts claiming a package couldn't be delivered, with a link prompting you to reschedule or even pay an import fee – the link often leads to malware.

- **Charity Scams:** Urgent texts appeal to your generosity during crises, with links leading to fake donation sites.

- **Account Verification Texts:** Claims your bank or login needs to be verified, directing you to a lookalike website to steal your info.

Protect Yourself: Identity Theft is Real (and It Sucks)

Identity theft is a massive headache that can mess up everything from your bank account to getting a loan. Protecting your info online and offline is critical. If someone does manage to swipe your information, it's stressful but not the end of the world. There are steps you can take.

1. Let all the credit reporting places (you know, the ones like Experian, Equifax, and TransUnion) or whichever credit bureaus are in your country know that your identity was stolen.

2. Contact any bank or company where something weird is happening with your accounts.

3. And report it to the authorities.

Identity Theft: It's Not Just for Your Parents

- **Ghosting Your Student Loans:** Imagine someone uses your info to open credit cards, racking up debt in your name. Suddenly, you're denied that student loan you desperately need because your credit score is trashed.

- **The Fake Job Nightmare:** Scammers can use your Social Security number to get jobs, sticking you with the tax bill on their income. Even worse, this could mess up your ability to get a legitimate job later.

- **Medical Mess-Ups:** Identity thieves can use your health insurance to get expensive prescriptions or procedures. Your medical records are mixed up with theirs, potentially affecting your future care.

Protecting Your Passwords: It's Like Guarding Your Digital Life

- **"123456" Isn't Cutting It:** Weak passwords are a welcome mat for hackers. Imagine someone logging into your social media and posting embarrassing stuff as you.

- **One Password to Rule Them All? Bad Idea:** If you reuse the same password for everything, a hacker cracks one account and suddenly has access to your bank, email, etc. It's a domino effect.

- **Password Managers: Your Secret Weapon:** They create crazy-strong, unique passwords for each site and remember them for you, like having a digital vault for your online identity.

Your digital legacy is important. It can affect everything from getting into college to landing your dream job. Taking care of it now sets you up for success later. Plus, who wants to deal with the mess of being careless online? Not you!

Data Breaches: When Companies Mess Up, It Affects You

- **Think "Target, But Worse":** Remember that huge data breach where millions of credit card numbers were stolen? Data breaches happen to stores, online games, and social media sites.

- **It's Not Your Fault, But It's Your Problem:** When your info's leaked, YOU have to watch for fraud, change passwords, and maybe even freeze your credit. It's a significant hassle. This happened to me when my personal details and password were leaked on the dark web. Even though Google claims it was a 'Non-Google Breach,' the hackers got into my website, replaced my content with fake-looking Chinese content, and redirected all my links to a scammer website claiming to sell clothes. Also, through Google, 89 passwords that I saved through Google to log into various websites were compromised and had to be changed. They also used my Debit card stored through Google to create fake Ads to run on a scam restaurant website and charged it to my card. This part really annoyed and upset me the most. I felt violated and very angry.

- **Steps to Take ASAP:** If a website you use gets breached, they should notify you. Immediately change your password there and anywhere else you reused it. Consider signing up for credit monitoring for a while.

Critical Points for Young Adults:

1. **You Are a Target:** Scammers go after young adults because they often have less established credit histories, giving fraudsters more time to operate undetected.

2. **This Affects Your Future:** Messy credit can make renting an apartment, buying a car, or getting your dream job harder.

3. **A Little Effort Goes a Long Way:** Taking these things seriously now can save you significant headaches (and money).

Protect Your Future

Shred sensitive documents, lock your mailbox, and be careful about sharing personal info. Regularly checking your financial statements and credit reports can help spot identity theft early.

Report and Educate

If you suspect a scam, report it. This helps protect others and disrupts the scammers. Educating yourself and others about common scams is also powerful. Knowing what to look for can prevent a lot of trouble.

"In general, pride is at the bottom of all great mistakes." - John Ruskin.

Red Flags: Too Good To Be True?

Managing your digital presence isn't just about privacy; it's about maintaining control of your personal and financial information in a world where these are increasingly meshed with your online identity. With careful monitoring and regular updates, you can ensure your digital self is as secure as your physical self.

If It Sparkles Too Bright, It's Probably Not Gold

The FOMO Trap: "Act NOW or miss this once-in-a-lifetime chance!" High-pressure sales tactics prey on your fear of missing out. Scammers know you're less likely to think logically if they get you emotional.

"Guaranteed" to Make You Rich: Any legitimate investment advisor will tell you there's always a risk. Research shows young adults are especially drawn to get-rich-quick schemes, and that's precisely what scammers exploit.

Crypto, Cash, But NO Credit Cards??: Legitimate businesses want to get paid! Demanding crypto, gift cards, wire transfers, or only cash are HUGE red flags. These methods make it nearly impossible to get your money back if scammed. It's always best to pay with Paypal, so you can get you're money back when things go wrong.

"This Deal is ONLY for Today!": Ever been pressured at a mall kiosk or online ad? They want you to buy before you can compare prices, read reviews, or realize that "miracle" hair growth oil is a total sham.

Here are Some Real-Life Examples Young Adults Face:

- **Fake Influencer Sponsorships:** "We love your vibe! D.M. us to collab." They offer free stuff, then ask for your credit card to "cover shipping" or lead you to a shady subscription trap.

- **"Easy Money" Jobs:** Stuffing envelopes, reshipping packages – often, these are fronts for money laundering or scams targeting other victims. You could unknowingly end up in legal trouble.

- **Romance Scams:** They sweep you off your feet online, then the sob stories start. Need money for a medical emergency, a plane ticket to visit you... These scammers are pros at emotional manipulation.

Key Takeaway: Trust your gut. If something feels too good to be true (or makes you slightly uneasy). Taking time to research ALWAYS beats losing money to a scam.

If You Think You've Been Scammed

How to Protect Yourself

1. **Slow Down, Be Suspicious:** Scammers rely on urgency. Before clicking anything, take a deep breath and analyze the message.

2. **Check for Typos and Weird Links:** Official communications are well-written. Bad grammar or unusual URLs are red flags.

3. **Go Direct:** Instead of clicking, contact the supposed company through their official website or phone number.

4. **Never Share Passwords or Banking Info:** Legitimate companies won't ask for this over text, email, or an unsolicited call.

You've Been Scammed... Now What?

Act Fast - It's Not Your Fault, But It Is Your Problem: The sooner you report a scam, the better your chances of potentially getting your money back or stopping further damage. Banks and credit card companies have fraud departments – use them!

The Credit Freeze: Block Those Thieves: Putting a freeze on your credit makes it harder for scammers to open new accounts in your name. It's a hassle but worth cutting off the damage. If you live in the U.S., visit <https://reportfraud.ftc.gov/> they have info on how to do this. If you live in the UK, visit <https://www.ncsc.gov.uk/collection/phishing-scams> or <https://www.actionfraud.police.uk/contact-us> for more info on how to report scams. If you don't live in either of these countries, then simply Google **"report scam+country where you live,"** and some results should tell you who exactly to report the scam or fraud.

Report, Report, Report: Websites like the FTC <https://reportfraud.ftc.gov/> and IC3 <https://www.ic3.gov/> track scam trends. Your report doesn't just help you; it helps protect others, too!

The Feels: It's okay to NOT Be okay: Getting scammed can mess with you. Anger, embarrassment, feeling stupid... It's totally normal. Research by websites like the AARP Fraud Watch Network <https://www.aarp.org/> shows scam victims often experience feelings similar to those who've been robbed or assaulted.

Key Takeaway: You are NOT dumb for falling for a scam. Scammers are manipulative and get better every day. By taking action and reporting the fraud, you're taking back your power.

<u>Action Points</u>

1. Make sure your current bank is secure.
2. Familiarize yourself with common scams relating to any hobbies or interests you may have.
3. Review your digital footprints and privacy settings for any companies you use and your social media accounts.
4. Practice safe online banking and browsing and Monitor your accounts regularly.

CHAPTER 10
Hustle Power - Side Gigs and Smart Income

"Make your life a masterpiece; imagine no limitations on what you can be, have, or do."

– Brian Tracy

L et's be real—money is crucial. Whether it's student loans, rising rent, or saving for that dream trip, finances can be a struggle. But here's the good news: you don't need a full-time job to boost your income. Side hustles can help you build your bank account and achieve your financial goals faster.

As the saying goes, *"Don't put all your eggs into one basket"*, when it comes to money and life - diversification is key! If the pandemic taught us one thing, you need to have multiple sources of income in today's world to diversify your earnings, provide a safety net, and accelerate your wealth accumulation to achieve financial independence at a younger age.

Example, My Side Hustle Journey

When I was a student, money was tight, and the struggle was real. Between classes, part-time jobs, and trying to have a social life, I needed extra cash. I discovered the gig economy and found myself earning more from my side hustles than my main job. These side gigs not only paid the bills but also boosted my confidence and skills.

"I made a lot of money doing side gigs in the past through freelance and flexible working agency apps."

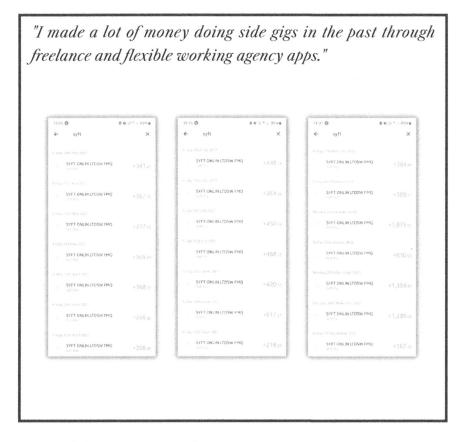

Unleashing Your Hustle Superpower

As a young adult, you have the energy and drive to take on the world. Side hustles are your secret weapon. Think of them as the Batman to your Bruce Wayne. By day, you're at work or in class; by night, you're out there making extra cash. Thanks to the internet and the gig economy, the possibilities are endless. So let's take a look at how to get started!

Skills-Based Hustles

Inventory Your Talents

Start by listing your skills. Are you great at graphic design, social media, or writing? Maybe you have a hobby like photography or coding that you can monetize. Identify your strengths and think of ways to turn them into side hustles. For example, if you're a graphic design major, consider offering freelance design services to local businesses or creating digital products like printables or templates. Whatever your skills, there's a way to monetize it.

Freelancing Platforms

Freelancing sites like Upwork, Fiverr, and Freelancer.com are great places to start. These platforms connect you with clients looking for specific skills. Create a profile, showcase your work, and start bidding on projects.

Example: Emma, the Graphic Designer

Emma, a graphic design major, created a profile on Upwork. She found clients needing logos, website designs, and social media graphics. As she completed projects and earned positive reviews, she landed higher-paying gigs and built long-term client relationships.

Freelancing platforms are perfect for:

- Writers and editors

- Coders and web developers

- Graphic designers

- Virtual assistants

- Online tutors and course creators

- Voiceover artists and video editors

- Photographers

- And tons more!

The Gig Economy

Apps like Uber, Lyft, GrubHub, and TaskRabbit offer flexible work opportunities. You can work when you have free time and earn extra cash. Just be mindful of expenses like gas and taxes.

The beauty of these gig apps is the flexibility - you can usually sign on to work whenever you have some spare time, whether a few hours after your day job, on weekends, or during school breaks and other commitments.

And thanks to the law of supply and demand, pay rates tend to be highest when everyone else wants to be out having fun - like Friday and Saturday nights. Ka-ching!

Fair warning: these gigs can be a grind, and you don't want to build a career around them. But they're a solid bet when you need to stack some cash quickly. Do the math on gas, vehicle wear and tear, and taxes to ensure you're coming out ahead.

Turning Hobbies into Hustles

Why not get paid for what you love? If you're into crafts, open an Etsy shop. If you love gaming, start streaming on Twitch. You can turn your hobbies into money-making ventures.

Example: John the Gamer: John loved gaming and started streaming on Twitch. His entertaining commentary and gameplay attracted a significant following. Now, he earns through donations, subscriptions, and sponsorships.

Creating Your Own Side Business

Ready to take it up a notch? Start your own side business. With e-commerce and online marketplaces, it's easier than ever. Whether it's a small catering business, a blog, or a local service, the sky's the limit.

Micro-Businesses

Micro-businesses are small, local businesses that can be run from home. They often have low start-up costs and can become profitable quickly.

Example: Custom Terrariums: If you're a plant enthusiast, start a micro-business creating custom terrariums. Source supplies in bulk, market on Instagram, and sell your creations.

The key to micro-business success is picking something you're fantastic at and enjoy doing that has a clear customer base willing to pay.

Some classic micro-business ideas:

- Baking and cake decorating for local events

- Tutoring and college essay coaching

- Personal shopping and styling for busy professionals

The possibilities are endless!

Local Service Businesses

Offer local services like house cleaning, lawn care, or tutoring. These businesses can take off with minimal start-up costs and provide steady income.

With creating your own side business, you are the boss and call the shots. If your business is doing really well financially and you are making more money with your side business than your actual job, you could even quit your normal 9-5 job and work on your business full time. Which for most people, this is the goal they are aiming for.

In the words of Successful Businessman, Kevin O'Leary, "*A Salary is the Drug They Give You to Forget Your Dreams*". This refers to employers offering their employees a steady salary to keep them complacent and potentially divert them from pursuing their dreams or entrepreneurial ambitions.

Social Media and Content Creation

If you're good at creating content, monetize it! Manage social media accounts, create YouTube videos, or start a blog. Build a following on any social media platform that you are already using such as TikTok, or Instagram and earn money through ads, sponsorships, affiliate marketing or selling merchandise.

Real-Life Example: Ali Abdaal, a former Doctor, YouTuber and Author

Ali Abdaal started a YouTube channel about productivity and studying. Consistent posting and valuable content grew his following, making him a multi-millionaire with successful online businesses. He then wrote a book to share his knowledge and experience called *'Feel Good Productivity.'* He didn't stop till he was successful, and his consistency and perseverance paid off.

> *"You do not have to be great to start, but you must start to be great." – Zig Ziglar*

The Passion Project Hustle

Turn your passion into a side hustle. Whether it's writing, music, or creating, pour your heart into it. Passion projects can be the most fulfilling and potentially lucrative.

Example: Sarah the Novelist: Sarah dreamed of writing a novel. She self-published her book on Amazon, promoted it on social media, and built a loyal fanbase. Now, she's a best-selling author with a steady income from her passion.

Here are a few more **examples of passion projects hustles** that have the potential to generate income:

- Blogging & Vlogging: Build a loyal audience with your unique voice and content over time.

- Podcasting + Audiobooks: Find your niche and share your thoughts, stories, and expertise.

- Online Courses: Teach others the valuable skills you know.

Smart Passive Income

Passive income is the dream—money that comes in with little ongoing effort. It requires initial work but can pay off over time. Create digital products, invest in stocks or real estate, or build a blog that generates ad revenue.

Building a System for Wealth Creation

In *"The Millionaire Fastlane"* by MJ DeMarco, a story about two brothers competing to build a pyramid illustrates different paths to wealth:

- **The Slowlane:** One brother carries each block up the pyramid, a slow, exhausting process. This represents working a 9-to-5 job, saving diligently, and hoping to retire comfortably after many decades.

- **The Fastlane:** The other brother builds a machine to lift the blocks, speeding up the process. This represents creating a business system or investment strategy that generates income with less direct effort, leading to faster wealth accumulation.

- **The Sidewalk:** Those on the sidewalk don't build anything. They might have short-term gains but lack a long-term strategy for wealth creation.

The key takeaway from the pyramid story is to think strategically and create systems that work for you. Focus on generating income through assets and businesses rather than just trading your time for money. Passive income is the way to go if you're tired of trading your time for money!

The "While You Sleep" Income Dream

Here's the thing - there's no 100% passive income unless you're inheriting stacks of cash or something. Every so-called "passive" income stream requires a significant upfront investment of time, effort, skills, or capital to get it up and running. The goal is to eventually reach a point where that initial work keeps paying off over a long period, with relatively minimal ongoing upkeep.

You need to adopt an abundance mindset to aid you in the hard times, and there will be hard times; that's just part of life. The key is to never give up. You don't need to pull yourself up by your bootstraps; no one gets anywhere far by themselves or do anything without some kind of help. You need to take advantage of the opportunities available as a young adult in the digital age and use your unfair advantage to get you where you want to go!

People who lack an abundance mindset tend and feel like they have to struggle to make it or to be worthy. These kinds of people tend to get in their own way and knock themselves out of opportunities which leads to them giving up too soon before they even have a chance to make it to success. Trust me, I use to be one of those people, before my financial awakening.

> *"Many of life's failures are people who did not realize how close they were to success when they gave up."*
>
> - Thomas A. Edison

Now, let's take a look at some smart passive income you can create.

1 | Digital Products

Create and sell digital products like eBooks, courses, digital art, printables, or templates on platforms like Etsy or Creative Market. Once made, they can be sold repeatedly with minimal effort.

If you're a subject matter expert on anything, from vegan meal planning to resumé writing to Pokémon card collecting, you could create:

- Ebooks

- Courses and video tutorials

- Templates and printables

- Apps and tools, *and so on!*

2 | Print on Demand Services (POD)

Use print-on-demand services to sell your designs on products like t-shirts and mugs. These services handle printing and shipping, so you don't need inventory.

How POD Works

- **You Design, They Do the Rest:** Upload your art to a POD website. They handle printing and shipping.

- **Zero Inventory, Zero Stress:** Products are only printed when sold, so no need for storage.

- **Your Brand, Your Way:** You control your online shop's look and feel.

POD isn't a get-rich-quick scheme. It's a side hustle that can turn into serious bucks. Let's talk about how:

- **Royalties:** Earn a cut from each sale, similar to passive income.

- **Unlimited Creativity:** Print on various products like t-shirts, phone cases, and mugs.

- **Social Media Power:** Use Instagram, TikTok, and Pinterest to build a following and drive sales.

Getting Started with POD

Here's your starter kit:

1. Choose Platforms: Use Printify, Printful, and Redbubble for easy setup

2. Create Standout Designs: If needed, hire freelancers from Fiverr or Upwork.

3. Find Your Niche: Target specific communities with your products.

4. Quality Control: Order samples to ensure high quality:

5. Use Mockups: Create professional product photos with tools like PlaceIt or Canva.

- Your art needs to stand out. Don't be afraid to experiment! If you struggle with design, find a freelancer (Fiverr and Upwork are great) to bring your vision to life. As Tiffany James, the CEO and founder of ModernBlkGirl, says, *"Hire for your weaknesses and not your comfortability."* Know what you do well and what you don't. For example, I'm not a graphics designer, so I hired a freelancer on Fiverr to do it for me.

6. Market Naturally: Share your products organically, avoiding spammy tactics.

POD is your ticket to turning your passions into something profitable – no warehouse or giant start-up cost is required. Start small, dream big, and most importantly, have fun expressing yourself along the way!

3 | Affiliate Marketing

Promote products and earn commissions on sales through your referral links. Build a following on social media or a blog and recommend products you love.

For example, let's say you're super passionate about ethical and cruelty-free beauty products. You could start an Instagram account where you post tutorials and honest reviews of your favorite clean makeup brands. As you grow your audience, you could join those brands' affiliate programs to make a percentage of any sales through the special shopping links in your posts. Ensure you only recommend stuff you genuinely love and use, not selling out to make a quick buck!

I run a blog <https://roshelinarush.com>, to help students and young adults improve their productivity and thrive. I earn through affiliate links, recommending products I believe in, and running ads on my site.

Affiliate marketing is not a get-rich-quick thing; it takes a lot of experimenting to figure out what resonates with your audience.

Build a loyal following who trust your recommendations for long-term success.

4 | Investing

Investing helps grow your wealth over time. Regularly invest a portion of your earnings into reliable, long-term investments to build wealth on autopilot.

The key takeaway is this: the earlier you can start investing, the more time you have to let compound interest work magic. Even small monthly contributions add up over time.

BEGINNER INVESTING TIPS

- **Employer 401k plan or equivalent:** Max out contributions to get the match—it's free money.

- **Roth IRA:** Open a Roth IRA and automate a monthly contribution, even if it's only $50/month to start.

- **Index Funds:** Don't get cute picking individual stocks - opt for low-fee index funds that track the overall market instead.

- **Robo-Advisors:** Consider financial technology (FinTech) "robo-advisor" apps like Acorns, Betterment, or Wealthfront to automate your investing if you're not confident picking your own portfolio.

- **REITs:** Research real estate investment trusts (REITs) to get a slice of that sweet rental income and appreciation.

Again, this is just the tip of the investing iceberg! Continue learning about smart long-term wealth-building strategies as you grow your side hustle empire.

Disclaimer: *This is for educational purposes only, not investment advice.*

While investing carries risks, it can also lead to passive income through dividends (that's, profits paid to shareholders) or the appreciation of your assets (an increase in the value of an asset over time). Platforms like Robinhood, Trading 212, and Acorns make investing more accessible and understandable. Start small and educate yourself! Always remember compounding interest may be your best friend when investing in a relationship with your money for the next 30, 40, or even 50 years. However, diversification is still a good friend of yours and will be there for you throughout your financial journey: so make sure you diversify!

Side Hustle Success Mindset

Now, I just threw a lot of side hustle strategies your way - it's a lot to take in! But before we wrap up, let's talk about mindset. Because here's the thing: you can have all the killer hustle ideas in the world, but if you don't have the right mental approach, you'll be spinning your wheels without gaining traction.

To succeed in the world of side hustles, you need to have the right mindset. You must be willing to take risks, be flexible, and adapt to changes.

Finding Your Hustle "Why": Clarify why you're side-hustling. Whether it's paying off debt, saving for a goal, or building more freedom, your "why" will keep you motivated. Here are a few active things you can do to stay motivated:

1. Write it down,

2. Post it on your mirror,

3. Make it your phone background

Whatever you need to do to keep your eye on the prize. Next up, let's talk about realistic expectations.

Realistic Expectations: Side hustles take time and effort. Don't expect overnight success. It takes trial and error and pure grit to gain momentum. Celebrate small wins and keep pushing forward.

So don't get discouraged if your first few Etsy listings flop, you only make $50 from your first freelance gig, or it takes you forever to build a decent affiliate income. That's totally normal! The key is not to let those early stumbling blocks derail you. Keep focusing on providing genuine value, honing your skills, and putting yourself out there consistently. Set realistic goals and celebrate your small wins along the way. The results will follow.

Balancing Act: Balancing a side hustle with other responsibilities can be tough. Manage your time wisely, communicate your goals, and take breaks to avoid burnout.

Pro Tips for Making It Work

- Block out non-negotiable hustle time in your schedule every week, and fiercely protect it.

- Get ruthless about eliminating time-wasters and energy-drainers from your life (doom-scrolling, flaky friends, over-committing to stuff you don't care about). I did this, and it was life-changing!

- Please communicate with your family and friends about your goals and enlist their support to free up your time and keep you accountable.

- Remember to take breaks and prioritize self-care! Hustling yourself into the ground helps nobody.

- Batch similar tasks and use productivity tools to streamline your workflow.

- Celebrate the small wins along the way, and cut yourself slack when things don't go perfectly.

It's a juggling act, but with careful planning and boundary-setting, you can make room for a lucrative side hustle without sacrificing your health, relationships, or sanity. Make sure to prioritize your time and energy, and don't be afraid to say no to commitments that drain your energy. Don't burn yourself out. Schedule hustle time wisely so it doesn't eat into your life.

Legal and Financial Advice

Stay on top of taxes, business licenses, permits, and financial management. Protect your hustle and keep it profitable.

Success doesn't happen overnight - it's all about consistently showing up, putting in the work, and staying focused on your goals. There will be ups and downs, wins and losses, epic breakthroughs, and demoralizing setbacks. But if you keep your eyes on the prize and your hustle game strong, there's no limit to how far your side gigs can take you.

Check out the YouTube video, *"How To Start A New Side Hustle | Step by Step Ultimate Beginners Guide"* located on the resources page to help you get started.

Action Points

1. Find ways to increase your income, such as starting a side hustle.

CHAPTER 11

Death and Taxes - The Inevitable Duo in Your Financial Journey

"In this world, nothing is certain but death and taxes"
- Benjamin Franklin.

L et's dive into a topic no one loves, but everyone needs to understand: taxes!

Understanding Taxes

Taxes are the government's way of collecting money to pay for essential public services—basically, things we all use, like roads, schools, and hospitals. Think of taxes as your membership fee for living in your country. It might seem like a drag to have to pay taxes, but they help keep everything running, meaning your sidewalks stay clear of garbage and your streets stay lit because your taxes keep the lights on.

How Taxes Work

When you start earning money, either through a job or a side hustle, a portion of that money goes to the government as taxes. The more you make, the more you pay. Each country has different rules, so check your government's website for details.

For example, in the UK, you can earn up to £12,570 tax-free (Gov.uk, 2024).

Different countries have different laws regarding this, so check yours on your Government website. However, you won't be expected to pay taxes in some countries. If you earn below a certain amount, you may be entitled to a personal allowance, which is the amount of income you can earn tax-free.

In the USA, it's the Internal Revenue Service (IRS) that's responsible for collecting federal income taxes. In the UK, the HM Revenue & Customs (HMRC) deducts the taxes from people's earnings. The U.S. and the UK have a progressive income tax system, meaning the more you earn, the more you pay in taxes. This mainly impacts the higher earners in society.

Different Types of Taxes

There are different kinds of taxes. The main ones that apply to regular people are:

1. Income Tax: Automatically deducted from your paycheck. Your country's tax authority will assign you a tax code so you know what tax bracket applies to you and what percentage of your paycheck will be deducted for taxes; this is displayed on your payslips. For instance, in 2024, if you're single and earn up to

$11,600, you're taxed at 10%, and If you're single and earn between $11,600 - $47,150, you'll be taxed at 12%.

Here is an example of how it works in real life:

In the USA, if you have $11,800 in taxable income in 2024, the first $11,600 is subject to the 10% rate, and the remaining $200 is subject to the tax rate of the next bracket (12%). (Smartasset, 2023). But don't worry.

- In the USA, your employer will provide a W-2 form at the end of the year, showing how much you earned and how much tax was deducted. You can get a tax refund if you've paid too much!

- For the UK, it's called the P60, which shows the tax you paid on your salary in the tax year (6 April to 5 April). You get a separate P60 for each job you do.

> **TIP:** Be sure to keep a copy of it, either digital or paper, just in case something goes wrong and you need evidence.

2. Sales Tax: A small amount added to things you buy at the store, like clothes or electronics. Most of us pay this one every time we buy something without even realizing it as it's 'included' in the price.

3. Property Tax: Owners of houses and land pay this based on what their property is worth.

Remember, the numbers mentioned here are specific to the tax year 2024 and are subject to change, pending any updates made.

Getting Help

Taxes can be confusing, but there are plenty of resources to help you. Always check the latest guidelines online and consult a tax professional if needed. It's important to pay your taxes correctly to avoid fines or even jail time for tax evasion.

When it comes to tax implications for your side hustle, you get taxed differently depending on the type of entity you are. For example, if you are a sole trader or a company, your taxes are not automatically deducted from a paycheck; you must fill out a tax return to pay this yourself.

The good news is that a side hustle opens up a world of potential tax deductions that can seriously reduce your tax bill. These include things like home office expenses (if you work from home), business equipment, supplies, website expenditures, and software fees. There are so many things that can be deducted!

Keeping Records

Keep detailed records of all your income and expenses. Use separate bank accounts and business credit cards to separate personal and business finances.

Estimated Quarterly Taxes

Since taxes aren't withheld from your paycheck, you'll need to pay estimated taxes in the tax year to the Internal Revenue Service (IRS) if you live in the US or the HM Revenue & Customs (HMRC), if you live in the UK. Every country has its Government department that collects taxes from people and businesses. You need to find out yours; a simple internet search should do the trick. Yes, it's a bit of a pain, but it beats getting slammed with a massive tax bill (and potential penalties) come tax season.

This helps avoid a huge tax bill and penalties at the end of the year.

Tools and Resources

If all of this makes your head spin, don't panic - there are tons of great resources out there to help you navigate the tax side of side hustling. Invest in accounting software like Wave or QuickBooks Self-Employed. Consider hiring a bookkeeper or tax professional, especially if you're new to this. Free resources like IRS.gov and SBA.gov offer guides and tutorials, so take advantage of them.

Don't let the tax stuff scare you from chasing your side hustle dreams. Stay informed, stay organized, and you'll be well on your way to financial success!

Remember what Charlie Brown said to Snoopy,

"We only live once, Snoopy".

His response was,

"Wrong! We only die once. We live every day!"

Action Points

1. Find out which government department collects taxes in your country.
2. Determine if you need to pay taxes on your side hustle using the ways described in the chapter.

CHAPTER 12

Retirement Planning - Investing to Make Money While You Sleep

"It's not how much money you make, but how much money you keep, how hard it works for you, and how many generations you keep it for."

- Robert Kiyosaki

Alright, my fellow money-savvy millennials and Gen Z-ers, let's talk about the secret sauce to building serious wealth: investing. The mere mention of the word might conjure up images of Wall Street suits yelling into phones or complex charts that look like hieroglyphics.

But I'm here to tell you that investing doesn't have to be some mysterious, intimidating thing reserved for the mega-rich.

In fact, it's one of the most potent tools we regular folks have for growing our money and securing our financial futures, even if you're starting with pocket change.

As young adults, we constantly seek ways to grow our money and secure our financial futures. Investing is a great way to do that, but it can seem intimidating and overwhelming.

In this chapter, we'll break down the basics of investing, debunk common myths, and provide practical tips for getting started.

What the Heck is Investing?

Investing is putting your money into assets with a good chance of increasing in value over time to earn a profit. It's like planting and nurturing a seed until it blossoms into a big, beautiful money tree (minus the watering and sunlight).

The goal is to grow your money while you sleep to achieve your financial goals and live the life you want.

Beyond the Savings Account

I know what you might think - "But I already have a savings account! Isn't that enough?" Well, my money-minded friend, while a savings account is a great place to park your emergency fund and short-term cash, it will only do a little to grow your wealth.

The interest rates are...well, let's say you won't buy that yacht soon. The interest rates on most savings accounts are laughably low - we're talking like 0.01% if you're lucky. At that rate, your money is just sitting there, twiddling its thumbs and losing value to inflation.

Inflation

Inflation is the rate at which the price of goods and services increases over time, which decreases the purchasing power of your money, making it harder to buy the same things with the same amount of money in the future.

For example,

While living in England, UK. I used to be able to buy three plantains for £1 ($1.30), but due to inflation, that same three plantains increased to £1.20 ($1.50), and then due to inflation, it rose again to 3 plantains for £1.50 ($2). Meaning you end up paying more for the exact same things.

This works the same way with your savings account, except with the money just sitting there and not gaining enough interest to overtake inflation, it begins losing its value.

Therefore, the same amount of money can no longer buy the same things at that price, so you end up paying more for the things you want.

Inflation can have a significant impact on your young financial life, in regards to:

- **Buying things:** The cost of everyday expenses like groceries, rent, gas, and entertainment can rise, making it challenging to maintain your lifestyle or afford necessities.

- **Saving money:** Inflation erodes the value of savings over time. Even if you save diligently, the money you've put aside might not be enough to cover future expenses, like a down payment on a house or car.

- **Investing:** Inflation also affects investments. If the returns on investments don't keep pace with inflation, the actual value of your investments decreases.

Unlike placing money into a savings account with a relatively low return, investing can significantly increase your capital over time, thanks to the power of markets and compounding interest. Investing takes your money and puts it into things with the potential to make more money in the long run.

It's not a fun process, to power-phrase one of the best investors of all time, Warren Buffett, *'investing is boring; if it feels fun, then you're doing it wrong'*.

Investments can take various forms, including stocks, bonds, real estate, and mutual funds, each with different risk levels and potential returns. Don't worry, we'll get to that later. First, look at the investments that allow you to earn a higher return on your money.

Stocks, Bonds, and Other Assets

You're not just handing your cash to the stock market and hoping for the best. You buy pieces of things, like:

- **Stocks:** Tiny pieces of ownership in companies

- **Bonds:** Lending money to companies or governments

- **Real Estate:** Investing in property

- **Index Funds:** A basket of stocks or bonds

- **ETFs:** Exchange-Traded Funds

- **Cryptocurrencies:** Digital currencies like Bitcoin

- **Other commodities:** Like gold (which always holds its value over time) or silver.

Think of it like a pizza. Stocks are like the toppings, bonds are like the crust, and real estate is like the pizza. Each has its own benefits and risks.

That's where investing comes in. When you invest, you put your money into stocks, bonds, real estate, or even precious metals like gold. Over the long haul, these assets have historically delivered much higher returns than a measly savings account - we're talking an average of 7-10% per year for a balanced portfolio.

EXAMPLE:

You have $1,000 to invest in a broadly diversified stock portfolio. On average, the stock market has returned about 10% per year over the past century. If you just let that $1,000 ride and never added another penny, in 30 years, it would grow to over $17,000! That's the magic of investing.

Ownership vs. Lending

One key concept to wrap your head around is the difference between ownership investments (like stocks) and lending investments (like bonds). When you buy stock in a company, you're basically becoming a part-owner of that business. If the company grows and becomes more profitable, the value of your shares should go up. On the flip side, your shares could lose value or become worthless if the company tanks.

On the other hand, you're acting as a lender with bonds. You give your money to a company or Government, and in exchange, they promise to pay you back with interest over a set period. Bonds tend to be less risky than stocks but generally deliver lower returns.

Most investors choose to build a diversified portfolio that includes a mix of stocks and bonds (along with other assets) to balance out risk and reward.

The Power of Compounding

Now, I'm about to let you in on the biggest secret weapon in the investing world: compound growth, also known as compound interest. Compounding is when the returns you earn on your investments start generating their own returns, which then generate their own returns, and so on, like a glorious snowball of money rolling down a hill. It starts small, but as it rolls, it grows and grows.

It's like a never-ending snowball fight!

Let's say you invest $100, and it grows 10% in a year. You now have $110. Next year, that $110 will increase by another 10%, that's $121. It might seem small initially, but the growth explodes over time!

The key to harnessing the power of compounding? Starting early and staying consistent. The longer your money has to grow, the more mind-boggling the results can be.

EXAMPLE:

Let's say you start investing $200 a month at age 20 and keep it up until you're 60, earning an average 7% annual return. By retiring, your portfolio would be worth a staggering $1.2 million! Let's say your friend waited until 30 to invest the same $200 a month. Even though they only started 10 years later, their portfolio at 60 would only be worth around $440,000 - still impressive, but only about a third of what you'd have by starting early!

Of course, these examples are simplified and not guaranteed - investment returns can vary wildly yearly. But the core principle holds true: the sooner you start investing, the more time you have to let compounding work its magic.

Busting Investing Myths

Now that you have a basic grasp of investing and why it's so powerful, let's bust some common myths that might hold you back from taking the plunge.

"You Need to Be Rich to Start": This is the biggest misconception - considering investing requires a lot of money. The truth is, you can start investing with as little as a few bucks a month! These days, tons of apps and platforms let you dip your toe in with super low minimums (we'll get into those more later). The key is to start somewhere, even if it feels like a drop in the bucket.

"Investing is Just Gambling": Watching stock prices bounce around day to day can feel a lot like rolling the dice in Vegas. But here's the thing: over the long run, the stock market has consistently increased. The key is to think long-term and block out the short-term noise. Historically, the likelihood of losing money in the stock market drops to nearly zero if you stay invested for 20 years or more. It's not guaranteed, but it's about as far from gambling as you can get.

"I Don't Have Time to Learn": Look, I know we're all busy AF these days - between work, school, side hustles, and trying to have some semblance of a social life. Who has time to become a financial expert? But thanks to modern technology, you don't have to spend hours poring over stock charts and financial reports to start investing. Robo-advisors and index funds (which we'll cover more in this chapter) have made it easier than ever to invest smartly without needing a PhD in finance.

"Day Trading Is the Way to Get Rich Quick": Repeat after me: trying to get rich quickly is a great way to lose all your money. Morgan Housel, the author of *"The Psychology of Money,"* expressed regrets about day-trading a bankrupt steel company when he was 19 years old, as he lost a lot of money and said he "didn't know why he thought day-trading a bankrupt steel company was a good idea."

I know those stories of day traders raking in cash are tempting, but for every one of those rare success stories, thousands of people crash and burn trying to time the market. Investing is a marathon, not a sprint - the real wealth comes from consistency and patience over the long haul.

Robo-advisors vs. DIY

Now that we've busted some investing myths, let's discuss how to start. One of your first decisions is whether to go the robo-advisor route or DIY your investments.

Robo-advisors Explained

Robo-advisors are precisely what they sound like - automated investing services using algorithms and software to build and manage your investment portfolio.

You fill out a questionnaire about your goals and risk tolerance, and the robo-advisor spits out a recommended portfolio mix and handles all the nitty-gritty trading and rebalancing for you. It's like having a robot money manager in your pocket!

Some popular robo-advisors include:

- Betterment

- Wealthfront

- Acorns

- SoFi Invest

- Ellevest

They are a low-cost, low-effort investment option suitable for beginners. They'll also manage your portfolio, so you don't have to worry about it.

Pros of Robo-advisors

- Low fees

- Customized investment plans

- Easy to use

- No minimum balance requirements

The main appeal of robo-advisors is that they make investing stupidly easy, even if you're starting with just a little bit of money. They take all the guesswork and legwork out of building a diversified portfolio, and most have super low fees compared to traditional financial advisors (usually around 0.25% of your account balance per year - so $25 on a $10,000 portfolio).

Robo-advisors are a great option if you're new to investing and want a "set it and forget it" approach. You can automate your contributions, kick back, and let the algorithms do their thing. On the flip side of the coin, you have DIY investing.

DIY Investing

If you're comfortable making investment decisions, DIY investing might be for you, where you take the reins and manage your portfolio. This involves opening a brokerage account with a company like Vanguard, Fidelity, or Charles Schwab and then hand-picking your investments. Remember, no one cares more about your money than you do.

The main benefit of DIY investing is that you have total control over what you invest in and can potentially save on management fees if you opt for low-cost index funds or ETFs (more on those in a second). It's also a great way to learn the ins and outs of investing and take ownership of your investments, since you're calling the shots.

When to Consider DIY

DIY investing can be a good fit if:

- You're interested in learning more about the nitty-gritty of investing

- You have a decent chunk of change to invest (think $10,000+)

- You're comfortable managing your own portfolio and doing your own research

- You want more control over your specific investments

That said, DIY investing does require more time and effort than going the robo-advisor route. You'll need to periodically rebalance your portfolio (adjusting your mix of investments to stay aligned with your goals) and ensure you're staying diversified. It's not rocket science, but it's not totally hands-off.

Real Estate Investing 101

Level up your investment game and dive into the exciting world of real estate investing!

I know what you might be thinking: "Real estate investing? Isn't that just for rich old dudes in suits?" But trust me, real estate is a powerful tool that can help anyone achieve financial freedom, regardless of background.

In this chapter, we'll break down the basics of real estate investing, explore the different ways you can get in on the action, and give you some practical tips and strategies to get started on your real estate journey. Let's go!

The Lowdown on Real Estate Investing

First, discuss why real estate is such a big deal when investing. Unlike stocks or bonds, real estate is a tangible asset - you can see, touch, and even live in it! This makes it a unique investment that offers two main ways to make money:

1. **Appreciation:** This is when your property's value increases over time. Just like a rare Pokémon card or a vintage comic book, real estate can become more valuable as time goes on, depending on factors like location, demand, and overall market conditions.

2. **Cash Flow:** You can make money from renting your property to tenants. Every month, you'll collect rent checks that can cover your mortgage payments and put extra cash in your pocket. It's like having a side hustle that pays you just for owning something!

Example:

Imagine you buy a cute little condo for $200,000 in an up-and-coming neighborhood. You put down 20% ($40,000) and rent it for $1,500 monthly. Your mortgage payment is $800, and you set aside $200 for maintenance and repairs. That leaves you with $500 a month in pure profit! Plus, over time, your condo's value increases as the neighborhood becomes more popular. After 10 years, your condo is worth $300,000, and you've made $60,000 in rental income. That's a total return of $160,000 on your initial $40,000 investment!

Different Ways to Invest in Real Estate

Okay, so you're pumped about the potential of real estate investing. But how do you actually do it? Well, there are a few different paths you can take:

1 | Buy and Hold: This is the most basic strategy, where you buy and rent a property out to tenants. You'll be responsible for things like finding renters, collecting rent, and handling repairs, but you'll also get to keep all the profits.

Action Step: Start browsing listings on sites like Zillow or Redfin to get a feel for prices and rental rates in your area. You can do a search online for your location. Make a list of neighborhoods you like and start crunching the numbers to see what you can afford.

2 | House Hacking: This is a clever strategy where you buy a multi-unit property, live in one unit, and rent out the others. It's a great way to start real estate investing while covering your living expenses!

Action Step: Look for duplexes, triplexes, or even houses with a basement apartment in your target neighborhoods. Run the numbers to see if the rental income from the other units could cover your mortgage and living costs.

3 | Fix and Flip: If you're handy with a hammer (or know someone who is), you could buy a fixer-upper, renovate it, and sell it for a profit. This more active approach requires some real estate savvy and elbow grease, but it can pay off big time.

Action Step: Watch some HGTV or Home Renovations shows to get a feel for the fix-and-flip process. Then, start researching distressed properties in your area and connecting with local contractors to get estimates on renovation costs.

4 | REITs: If you're not quite ready to buy a physical property, you can still invest in real estate through Real Estate Investment Trusts (REITs). These companies own and manage income-generating properties, and you can buy shares in them just like you would with a stock.

Action Step: Research popular REITs like American Tower, Prologis, or Equinix to see which ones align with your investment goals. You can buy REIT shares through your regular brokerage account.

Tips for Getting Started in Real Estate Investing

Alright, so you've got the basics down, and you're ready to dive in. Here are a few practical tips to help you get started on your real estate investing journey:

1. Educate yourself: Before you start throwing money at properties, take some time to learn the ins and outs of real estate investing. Read books, listen to podcasts, and connect with other investors in your area. The more you know, the better equipped you'll be to make smart decisions.

2. Crunch the numbers: Real estate investing is all about the math. Before buying a property, ensure you understand all the costs involved (down payment, mortgage, taxes, insurance, repairs, etc.) and how much rental income you can realistically expect. Use online calculators or spreadsheets to run the numbers and ensure the deal makes sense.

3. Get creative with financing: Coming up with a down payment can be tough, especially if you're starting out. But there are ways to get creative with financing, like partnering with other investors, using an FHA loan (which allows for lower down payments), or even borrowing from your 401(k). Don't let a lack of cash hold you back from getting started.

4. Build a team: Real estate investing can be a lot of work, but you don't have to do it alone. Build a team of professionals who can help you along the way, like a real estate agent, a property manager, a contractor, and a lender. Having a solid support system will make the process a lot smoother and less stressful.

5. Think long-term: Real estate investing is a marathon, not a sprint. Don't expect to get rich overnight or make a killing on your first deal. Instead, focus on building a portfolio of solid, cash-flowing properties over time. With patience and persistence, you can create a steady stream of passive income that can last a lifetime.

You don't have to become a real estate mogul overnight. The most important thing is to start taking action, even for small steps like researching your local market or saving up for a down payment.

Real estate investing is a powerful tool for building long-term wealth and achieving financial freedom. By getting started now, while you're young and have time on your side, you can set yourself up for a bright economic future.

So what are you waiting for? Get out there and start exploring the exciting world of real estate investing! With a little knowledge, creativity, and hustle, you can make your real estate dreams a reality.

> **Disclaimer:** Real estate investing involves risk and is not suitable for everyone. Always research and consult with a financial professional before making any investment decisions.

Your First Investment: Taking the Plunge

I think every employee has had that dream of giving the 'middle finger' to the taxman every time we look at the amount that gets deducted from our paychecks. So let's look at some ways that we can quietly and passively build up our wealth and invest in our future with tax advantages while screwing the taxman over at the same time.

Passive Investing

401K, Retirement, or Workplace Pension Scheme: Many people, specifically employees, need to learn that their very first investment is often their retirement or pension through a 401K or workplace pension plan, a tax-advantaged retirement account offered by your employer.

When you start working, by law, your employer has to automatically enroll you in a retirement or state pension scheme (which you can opt out of later if you want). You need to set this up with your employer; it's often done at the start of your employment before your first payday.

Sometimes, your employer will match the contribution. This means for every dollar deducted from your paycheck and put into your 401K or another pension scheme, they will match it exactly or contribute at least a percentage of the amount. This is you investing in your future without putting in any money upfront, and it will continue to grow. If you keep working, the account will fill up with free money from your job over time.

I won't just rely on the Government of my country to fund my retirement. Especially when in the UK, they keep pushing back the retirement age to keep more people in work for longer. As of 2024, you have to wait till you're 66 years old to retire, but this is set to rise again (Gov.uk, 2024). To check the retirement age for your country, search the internet or go to your Government's website and look at what age you're expected to keep working unless you have enough money to retire early.

Roth IRA: Another way to passively invest in your future is to open a Roth IRA account, which is an after-tax investment account that allows you to put money in without the investment growth getting taxed when you're ready to take it out down the line. The maximum amount you can put into your Roth IRA as of 2024 is $7,000 if you're younger than 50. You need to determine the maximum you can put in if you have a similar account but live outside the US. Take advantage of this by trying to put the MAXIMUM in each year.

Health Savings Account (HSA): Another excellent retirement investing account is the HSA. As of 2024, you can put $4,150 for individuals per year. It's a tax-free account, but the only catch is that you can only withdraw money from it early, if it's for health-related expenses up to the age of 65. Otherwise, those funds get taxed as ordinary income and the IRS may impose a 20% penalty for using the money for non-qualified expenses.

Okay, so you're pumped to start actively investing yourself - amazing! Here's how to actually take that first step.

Setting a Small Goal

First, set a realistic starter goal for how much you want to invest. It could be as simple as investing $100 in a broad market index fund or buying shares in a company you believe in. Make it achievable and celebrate when you reach it. If funds are tight, that might be as little as $100 or even $20 - that's fine! The key is to start building the habit. If you have more cash, consider aiming for a few thousand. But don't pressure yourself - every dollar counts.

Building on this, you can also set SMART Goals for your first investment.

Example of a SMART Investment Goal:

"I want to spend 1 hour every weekday to learn about investing, specifically index funds, and start investing in the next three months."

- **Specific:** I want to gain a solid understanding of index funds and open a brokerage account for this type of investing.

- **Measurable:** I will learn by reading two recommended books and completing an online course on index funds.

- **Achievable:** I will dedicate one hour each weekday to my investing education.

- **Relevant:** Index funds provide a low-cost and diversified way to begin investing.

- **Time-bound:** I aim to complete my learning and open an account within three months.

Index Funds for Beginners

If you're going the DIY route, one smart place to begin is with index funds. Index funds are baskets of investments (like stocks or bonds) that track a particular market index, like the S&P 500 in the US or the FTSE 100 in the UK. These are the top 500 performing companies in the US or the top 100 in the UK.

They offer instant diversification and tend to have much lower fees than actively managed mutual funds.

Some popular beginner index funds:

- Vanguard Total Stock Market Index Fund (VTSAX)

- Fidelity ZERO Total Market Index Fund (FZROX)

- Schwab Total Stock Market Index Fund (SWTSX)

These funds are recommended for education purposes only and should not be taken as financial advice. They give you broad exposure to the US and UK stock markets, so you're not putting all your eggs in one basket. They're a great core building block for any portfolio.

Choosing a Platform

Whether you choose a robo-advisor or DIY approach, you'll need to choose a platform or brokerage to open your account and start investing. Some things to consider:

- Minimum investment requirements (how much you need to get started)

- Management fees (how much you'll pay in annual fees)

- User experience (is the platform easy to navigate and use?)

- Investment options (does the platform offer the specific investments you're interested in?)

Choose a platform that fits your needs. For robo-advisors, some top options are Acorns, Wealthfront, and Betterment. Check out Vanguard, Fidelity, Charles Schwab, or newer players like

Robinhood or M1 Finance for DIY investing.

Celebrating the Milestone

Once you've taken that first plunge and made your first investment (woohoo!), take a moment to celebrate. You've just taken a massive step towards building long-term wealth and financial security.

Sure, it might just be a small slice of your paycheck or side hustle earnings but don't underestimate the power of starting early and staying consistent. If you can commit to steadily increasing your contributions over time (like bumping up your investment by 1% of your income each year), you'll be amazed at how quickly your wealth can snowball and grow.

And hey, don't get discouraged if the stock market has some wild swings in the short term - that's normal! Just keep your eyes on the long game, trust the magic of compound returns, and know your future self will give you a huge high five.

Remember: Investing is a marathon, not a sprint. Get educated, start small, be patient, and let your money make you money!

You've got this, my money-crushing friend! Here's to letting your money work hard for you so you can enjoy more of the good stuff in life. Cheers to that! Always remember that wealth is something you don't see when it comes to money and investing.

It's not the flashy car or designer handbag but the stock portfolio quietly growing in value. It's not the impulsive spending but the disciplined saving and budgeting.

True wealth often lies in the financial choices that aren't on display – the emergency fund providing peace of mind, the retirement account building for the future, and the debt-free life allowing flexibility and opportunity.

Remember, the most impressive wealth might be the least noticeable at first glance.

Action Points

1. Scan the QR Code or Click to Download the **Investment Quiz** to find your investment strategy.
2. Watch the 'Millionaire Payday Routine' YouTube video to break free from financial stress on Payday. URL:< https://www.youtube.com/watch?v=JRH-enfeY2w>
3. Watch the YouTube video, 'Vanguard Index Funds: A Complete Beginner's Guide to Investing'. URL: <https://www.youtube.com/watch?v=PVgpKaXj0fk>

KNOW YOUR STRATEGY, KNOW WHERE TO START!

CHAPTER 13

Exchange Traded Funds (ETFs) - Your New Best Friends in Investing

"Those of you who make investments outside of any retirement accounts are absolutely crazy if you are using actively managed funds rather than ETFs."

- Suze Orman

If you're ready to level up your investing game, it's time to get cozy with three little letters that pack a big financial punch: ETF. No, I'm not talking about an alien species or a trendy new social media app (though that would be cool). I'm talking about Exchange Traded Funds - the investment tool that's been taking the finance world by storm.

Think of ETFs like the Netflix of investing. Instead of buying individual stocks or bonds (which is like trying to pick the one-hit show in a sea of mediocrity). ETFs let you invest in a whole bundle of securities with one click. It's like getting access to an entire library of financial assets without having to do all the research and legwork yourself.

So grab your avocado toast, put on your favorite podcast, and let's dive into the world of ETFs!

What the Heck is an ETF?

Picture this: you're at your local fancy coffee shop, sipping on an overpriced latte, when you overhear some finance bros throwing around terms like "diversification," "passive investing," and "expense ratios." Your ears perk up - these are essential investing concepts, but you must figure out how they all fit together. Enter ETFs - the investment vehicle that combines all these ideas in one neat, tidy package.

At its core, an ETF is an investment fund that owns a bunch of underlying assets (like stocks, bonds, commodities, or even real estate) and divides ownership into shares. Those shares trade on stock exchanges (just like individual stocks) and can be bought and sold throughout the day.

In plain English, ETFs let you invest in a whole collection of stuff with a single transaction. It's like buying a pre-made investment buffet instead of trying to cook up a portfolio from scratch.

EXAMPLE:

Let's say you're interested in investing in the tech industry, but you're not sure which individual companies to pick. Instead of spending hours researching and agonizing over which stocks to buy (and potentially putting all your eggs in one basket), you could invest in a technology-focused ETF.

This ETF might own shares in giants like Apple, Microsoft, and Amazon and smaller, up-and-coming tech companies. By buying a share of this ETF, you instantly get exposure to the entire tech industry without having to bet on individual winners and losers.

The Beauty of Diversification

One of the most significant advantages of ETFs is that they offer instant diversification. And no, I'm not talking about the kind of "diversification" that happens when you mix Sour Patch Kids with buttered popcorn at the movie theater (though that's also a bold move).

Diversifying means spreading your money across many investments, so you're not putting all your eggs in one basket. Your entire portfolio won't be dragged down if one investment takes a nosedive.

ETFs make diversification a breeze because they allow you to invest in hundreds (or even thousands) of securities with a single purchase. Instead of trying to build a diversified portfolio by buying individual stocks and bonds (which can be time-consuming and expensive), you can get broad market exposure with just one or two well-chosen ETFs.

Example:

Imagine you have a spare $1,000 that you want to invest. You could diversify by buying shares in 20 different companies across various industries, but that would involve a ton of research, not to mention trading fees for each individual transaction.

Alternatively, you could put that $1,000 into an ETF that tracks the S&P 500 index (like the famous S.P.Y. or V.O.O. ETFs). These ETFs own shares in 500 of the largest U.S. companies, spanning technology, healthcare, and energy sectors. You've instantly diversified across the U.S. stock market with a single purchase. Boom, mic drop.

Passive Investing Made Easy

Another major selling point of ETFs? They make passive investing accessible to the masses.

For those who slept through Econ 101, passive investing is a strategy where you aim to match the performance of a particular market index (like the S&P 500 or the Dow Jones Industrial Average) rather than trying to beat the market by picking individual stocks.

The logic behind passive investing is pretty simple. Over the long run, most actively managed funds (where hotshot portfolio managers try to outsmart the market) fail to consistently outperform basic index funds. By investing in a low-cost index ETF, you can get returns similar to the overall market without paying hefty fees for fancy fund managers.

ETFs have made passive investing easier than ever because they offer a cheap, convenient way to track popular indexes. Instead of trying to cobble together your own index fund by buying hundreds of individual stocks, you can snag an index ETF and call it a day.

EXAMPLE:

You're scrolling through your favorite finance subreddit when you see a heated debate about whether investing in actively managed mutual funds or passive index funds is better. The active fans swear their fund managers have the secret sauce to beat the market, while the passive crew says it's all about keeping costs low and riding the market waves.

After researching, you dip your toes into the passive investing pool. You open up a brokerage account and buy shares in a few core index ETFs: one that tracks the total U.S. stock market, covers international stocks, and provides exposure to the U.S. bond market. Congrats, you're now a bona fide passive investor!

You'll want to invest in the U.S. stock market because it's one of the biggest stock markets in the world. And don't worry. If you're thinking that you have to live in the U.S. to get access to invest in the U.S. stock market, you don't have to! There are a few different ways for non-U.S. investors to open an international account. For one, you can open an account in your country of residence that offers access to the U.S. stock market.

Low Costs, High Impact

I know what you might think: "Sure, ETFs sound great, but what's the catch? There's gotta be some hidden fees or gotchas, right?"

Well, my financially savvy friend, I've got some good news for you: one of the biggest benefits of ETFs is their low-cost structure.

Because ETFs are passively managed (meaning they try to match an index rather than paying a fancy fund manager to pick stocks), they tend to have much lower expense ratios than actively managed mutual funds. The expense ratio is the annual fee a fund charges its shareholders, expressed as a percentage of its total assets.

While actively managed funds often have expense ratios of 1% or higher (which might not sound like much but can seriously erode your returns over time), many popular ETFs have 0.1% or less expense ratios. That means you get to keep more of your hard-earned returns in your pocket instead of lining the pockets of Wall Street fat cats. You don't have to see the movie 'The Wolf of Wall Street' to know what I'm talking about.

Example:

Let's say you're trying to choose between investing in an actively managed mutual fund with an expense ratio of 1% or a comparable index ETF with an expense ratio of 0.1%.

If you invested $10,000 in each fund and earned an annual return of 7% over 30 years, here's how the expenses would shake out:

- In the mutual fund, you'd pay a whopping $6,243 in fees, leaving you with a final balance of $57,435.

- In the ETF, you'd pay only $789 in fees, leaving you with a final balance of $73,967.

That's a difference of over $16,000 just by choosing a low-cost ETF! Imagine what you could do with that extra cash - pay off student loans, save for a down payment on a house, or finally take that dream trip to Bali.

Liquidity and Flexibility

Another awesome thing about ETFs? They offer liquidity and flexibility that traditional mutual funds just can't match.

Liquidity refers to how easily you can buy or sell an investment without affecting its price. ETFs are highly liquid because they trade on stock exchanges throughout the day, like individual stocks. That means you can buy or sell ETF shares whenever the market is open, and you'll always know the exact price you're getting.

Contrast that with mutual funds, which are only priced once daily (after the market closes) and can only be bought or sold at that price. If you want to sell your mutual fund shares, you have to wait until the end of the day to see what price you'll get - and if the market takes a nosedive in the meantime, you're out of luck.

ETFs also offer more flexibility in terms of how you trade them. Because they trade like stocks, you can do things like place limit orders (setting a specific price at which you're willing to buy or sell) or even short-sell ETFs if you think their price will go down.

EXAMPLE:

Picture this, you wake up one morning to the news that the Federal Reserve has announced a surprise interest rate hike. You know this will likely cause some market volatility, and you want to take advantage of any potential dips in stock prices.

With ETFs, you could log into your brokerage account and place a limit order to buy shares of your favorite index ETF at a specific price (say, 5% below the current market price). If the market does dip to that level, your order will be executed automatically, allowing you to scoop up shares at a discount. Try doing that with a mutual fund!

Building Your ETF Portfolio

Okay, so you're sold on the awesomeness of ETFs. But how do you build an ETF portfolio that works for you?

First, consider your investment goals and risk tolerance. Are you saving for retirement a down payment on a house, or just looking to grow your wealth over the long term? How much volatility are you willing to stomach in pursuit of higher returns?

Based on your answers, you'll want to choose a mix of ETFs that provide exposure to different asset classes (like stocks, bonds, and real estate) and geographic regions (like the U.S., developed international markets, and emerging markets).

A well-diversified ETF portfolio might include:

- A broad U.S. stock market ETF (like VTI or S.C.H.B.)

- An international stock ETF (like V.X.U.S. or I.X.U.S.)

- A US bond ETF (like BND or A.G.G.)

- A real estate ETF (like V.N.Q. or S.C.H.H.)

The exact mix will depend on your specific goals and risk tolerance - a more aggressive investor might have a higher stock allocation. In contrast, a more conservative investor might tilt more toward bonds.

EXAMPLE:

Let's say you're 25 years old and just starting to invest for retirement. You're comfortable with some market volatility, but you also want to ensure your portfolio is well-diversified.

You decide to build a simple three-fund portfolio using ETFs:

- 60% in a U.S. total stock market ETF (like VTI)

- 30% in an international stock ETF (like V.X.U.S.)

- 10% in a U.S. bond ETF (like BND)

This portfolio gives you broad exposure to the global stock market, with a small allocation to bonds to provide stability. As you get closer to retirement, you might shift more of your portfolio towards bonds to reduce risk.

The ETF Edge

So, there you have it - the lowdown on ETFs and why they're a must-have in any savvy investor's toolkit. To recap:

- ETFs offer instant diversification, allowing you to invest in hundreds or thousands of securities with a single purchase.

- They're a cheap and easy way to get exposure to broad market indexes, making passive investing accessible to everyone.

- ETFs have lower costs than actively managed mutual funds, so more of your money can grow over time.

- They're highly liquid and flexible, allowing you to trade throughout the day and use advanced order types.

- Building a well-diversified ETF portfolio can help you achieve your long-term investment goals while managing risk.

Disclaimer: I am not giving you financial advise; this is just for education purposes only. **Always do your own research, never**

invest more than you can afford to lose, and stay the course even when the market gets wild.

Your future self (and your wallet) will thank you.

Action Points

1. Complete the ETF Challenge. Scan the QR Code or Click to Download the ETF Portfolio Building Challenge

---

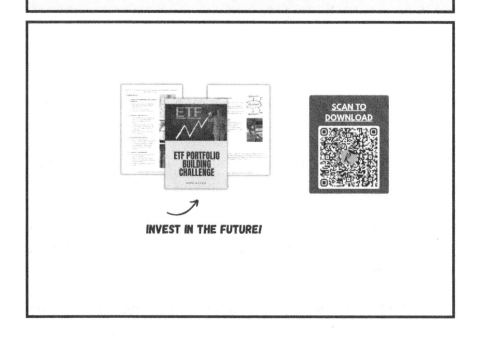

CHAPTER 14

Understanding Digital Currency - The Future of Money is Here

"If the cryptocurrency market overall or a digital asset is solving a problem, it's going to drive some value."
- Brad Garlinghouse

H ey there, tech-savvy Gen Z-ers and millennials! It's time to dive into the exciting and sometimes confusing world of digital currency. Whether you're a crypto-curious newbie or a blockchain enthusiast, this chapter is your ultimate guide to navigating the rapidly evolving landscape of virtual money. I've got you covered from Bitcoin to CBDCs (don't worry; I'll explain what those are).

So grab your smartphone, fire up your digital wallet, and let's explore the future of finance together!

Basics of Digital Currency

First things first, let's define "digital currency." Simply put, digital currency is any money that exists electronically without physical notes or coins. Think of it as the internet version of cash.

You can't hold it in your hand, but you can use it to buy things online, like a new pair of sneakers, or to split the bill for avocado toast with your friends. You can even use it to invest. Now that we know the basics, let's look at the available types.

Cryptocurrencies: The O.G.s of Digital Money

Cryptocurrencies are the most well-known type of digital currency. You've likely heard of Bitcoin, the grand daddy of all cryptos, but there are thousands of others, like Ethereum, Litecoin, and even Dogecoin, which started as a joke but now has a strong community behind it.

So, what makes cryptocurrencies different from regular money? For starters, they're decentralized, meaning they're not controlled by any government or financial institution. Instead, they run on a technology called blockchain that allows for secure, transparent transactions without needing a middleman.

EXAMPLE:

Think of cryptocurrencies as the rebel outcasts of the money world. They don't play by the rules of traditional banking systems—they're all about financial freedom! Using a digital wallet, you can buy, sell, or trade cryptocurrencies from your phone. No bank branches or paperwork is required.

Even platforms like PayPal accept cryptocurrencies as payment. Customers in the U.S. (excluding Hawaii) can use PayPal to transact with Bitcoin, Ethereum, Litecoin, and Bitcoin Cash. More countries are likely to be added over time.

As we move towards a cashless, digital society, the question remains: will governments and banks adapt to the changing times or get left behind?

Central Bank Digital Currencies (CBDCs): The New Kid on the Block

Governments and central banks aren't letting cryptocurrencies steal all the spotlight. Enter CBDCs—digital versions of traditional fiat currencies (like the U.S. dollar) backed and issued by central banks.

CBDCs offer the convenience of digital transactions with the stability of government-backed money. Countries like China, Sweden, and the Bahamas are already exploring or implementing CBDCs. The Bahamas' Sand Dollar and China's Digital Currency Electronic Payment (DCEP) are examples of CBDCs aiming to maintain financial stability against private cryptocurrencies.

Example:

Imagine paying your taxes, receiving government benefits, or buying coffee using a digital version of the U.S. dollar, all from a single app on your phone. That's the potential of CBDCs—making financial transactions faster, cheaper, and more accessible for everyone.

However, think of banks and governments as businesses. They operate to make money, and with the rise of digital currencies, they'll fight for relevance, which means controlling how we spend, save, and invest. This could impact how they use digital currencies to maintain control over us.

Money has always been in the hands of the rich and powerful, but the internet has leveled the playing field. Anyone with an internet connection can become rich and influential. While there's plenty to go around, not everyone thinks this way. We still need people in manual labor jobs until A.I. and robots can fully take over. This reality contributes to social classes: the poor, the middle class, and the wealthy.

People with money don't want to work manual labor jobs. When was the last time you saw a rich person working a manual labor job to cover their bills? It just doesn't happen.

Many people are jumping on the digital currency bandwagon because it's new and seen as the future of money, immune to inflation. So, if you're interested in building your wealth through digital currencies, now's the time to try it.

Digital Wallets: Your Key to the World of Digital Currency

So you're excited about digital currency, but how do you store and spend it? Enter the digital wallet—your trusty sidekick in the world of virtual money.

How Digital Wallets Work

A digital wallet is your key to the crypto kingdom. Unlike a physical wallet, it's a software-based system that securely stores your payment information and passwords. It's an app or software program that stores your digital keys, proving you own your cryptocurrency and letting you make transactions.

There are many digital wallets, each with different features and security levels.

Some popular options for storing cryptocurrencies include:

- Coinbase Wallet

- Mycelium

- Exodus

- MetaMask

- Ledger Nano X (a hardware wallet for extra security)

When choosing a digital wallet, consider ease of use, compatibility with different cryptocurrencies, and security features like two-factor authentication and multi-sig functionality (requiring multiple people to approve transactions).

EXAMPLE:

Let's say you're ready to dive into Bitcoin. You download the Coinbase Wallet app, create an account, and voilà—you have a shiny new Bitcoin wallet! You can buy Bitcoin using traditional money or receive it as payment for a freelance gig. When you're ready to spend your Bitcoin, whip out your phone, scan a Q.R. code, or enter a wallet address, and hit send. Easy peasy, digital squeezy!

Digital wallets don't just store cryptocurrencies but also your money digitally in general. Nowadays, we store our cards digitally on our phones and can pay for things with a simple tap of our phone to the card reader.

Contactless Payments

Contactless payments transform the way we pay, offering speed and convenience. Tap your contactless-enabled card or smartphone over the payment terminal, and voilà! The transaction is complete, thanks to short-range wireless technologies like NFC (Near Field Communication).

No swiping, no PIN entering, and no fumbling with cash—just a quick tap, and you're on your way!

Securing Your Digital Dough

With great digital power comes great responsibility. Just like you wouldn't leave your physical wallet unattended at a crowded coffee shop, you must protect your digital currency from hackers and thieves. Your digital wallet is your lifeline—protect it!

To secure your digital wallet, follow these best practices:

1. Use a strong, unique password and enable two-factor authentication (2FA).

2. Store large amounts of cryptocurrency in a hardware wallet, which is a physical device that stores your private keys offline.

3. Never share your private keys or seed phrases (a list of words to recover your wallet) with anyone. And definitely don't post them on social media!

4. Keep your software and apps up to date.

5. Be wary of phishing scams and fake websites/apps that try to trick you into entering your wallet credentials. Always double-check URLs and only download wallets from official sources.

EXAMPLE:

Picture this: you're chatting with a cute Tinder match who suddenly starts asking about cryptocurrency. Red flag alert! If someone you don't know is pressuring you to invest in a specific crypto or share your wallet info, run for the digital hills. That's a classic crypto scam. No matter how charming or convincing they are, never give your private financial details to strangers on the internet. Your digital currency is like your underwear—keep it private!

The Blockchain Revolution

It's time to talk about the backbone of the digital currency world: blockchain. It sounds like something out of a sci-fi movie, but trust me—this tech will change everything.

At its core, a blockchain is a decentralized digital ledger that records transactions across a network of computers. Picture a giant, virtual notebook shared and updated in real-time by thousands worldwide. Each "block" in the chain contains a bunch of transactions, and once a block is added, the transactions can't be altered or deleted.

So why is this revolutionary? Because it allows for secure, transparent transactions without the need for intermediaries like banks or governments. No more waiting days for money transfers to clear or paying hefty fees to financial institutions.

With blockchain, transactions are fast, cheap, and tamper-proof.

However, the potential applications of blockchain go way beyond just digital currency. This technology could transform everything from supply chain management to voting systems to healthcare records. By providing a secure, decentralized way to store and share data, blockchain can increase efficiency, reduce fraud, and give individuals more control over their personal information.

Examples:

- Imagine tracking the journey of your fair-trade coffee beans from the farm to your cup, ensuring farmers are paid fairly and no shady middlemen are skimming profits. That's the power of blockchain in supply chain transparency.

- Picture having complete control over your personal health data, easily sharing it with doctors or researchers as you see fit. No more worrying about insurance companies or big pharma misusing your information. Blockchain could make that a reality.

- Blockchain could also revolutionize voting, creating tamper-proof digital voting systems that increase accessibility and trust in democratic processes. No more dealing with voter fraud accusations!

The possibilities are endless, and we're just scratching the surface of what blockchain can do. As a smart, forward-thinking young adult, it's worth keeping an eye on this space and considering how blockchain might shape your career and financial future.

We've covered a lot: the basics of digital currency, from

cryptocurrencies to CBDCs to digital wallets and blockchain. It can seem overwhelming, but trust me—this stuff will be a big deal in the coming years.

As digital natives, you're uniquely positioned to take advantage of this new financial frontier. Whether you're interested in investing in cryptocurrencies, building blockchain-based applications, or just staying informed about the future of money, now's the time to start exploring and learning.

But remember—with great digital power comes great responsibility. Always do your own research, stay vigilant about security, and never invest more than you can afford to lose.

The digital currency world is still a bit like the Wild West—exciting and full of potential but also risky and uncertain. So stay curious, stay smart, and stay alert about the digital money revolution.

Who knows—maybe one day you'll be telling your grandkids how you were one of the early adopters of the currency that changed the world!

"The hardest part is starting. Once you get that out of the way, you'll find the rest of the journey much easier."
- Simon Sinek

Action Points
1. Scan the QR Code or Click to Download the **Digital Currency Scavenger Hunt** activity
2. Secure your Digital wallet.

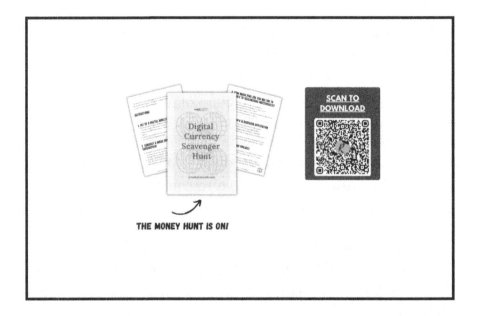

Inspire a New Young Adult to Learn About Money!

Now you have everything you need to prepare for major life expenses, make smart financial decisions, and gain independence. It's time to pass on your newfound knowledge and show other readers where they can find the same help.

Simply by leaving your honest opinion of this book on Amazon, you'll show other young adults where they can find the information they're looking for, and pass their passion for learning how to level up their finances forward.

Feeling the love and don't want our journey together to end? Visit <https://roshelinarush.com> for more free, helpful content to help you level up your young adult life. I'm committed to helping you and others like you reach personal and financial goals.

Thank you so much for reading this book. Knowing that my message is reaching those who need it most fills my heart with gratitude. I can't wait to hear about your success.

Thank you, from the bottom of my heart.

— Roshel Waite

Conclusion

C ongratulations, you've reached the end of this exhilarating journey through the world of personal finance. By now, your mind is probably buzzing with newfound knowledge, innovative ideas, and a burning desire to take control of your financial destiny.

Throughout this book, we've tackled some of the most crucial aspects of money management in the digital age. We started by unraveling the mysteries of your money mindset and exploring how your unique experiences and beliefs shape your financial decisions. You've learned to distinguish between needs and wants, to resist the siren song of instant gratification, and to harness the power of mindful spending.

But we didn't stop there. We delved into the art of budgeting, transforming it from a dreaded chore into an empowering tool for achieving your craziest dreams. You discovered the magic of paying yourself first, automating your savings, and watching your wealth grow through the power of compound interest.

As we ventured into credit scores, debt management, and side hustles, you gained the confidence to navigate these complex landscapes efficiently. You now understand how to build and maintain a stellar credit score, break free from the chains of bad debt, and supercharge your income with your unique skills and passions.

We then embarked on a thrilling exploration of the investing universe, demystifying concepts like stocks, bonds, and ETFs. You learned how to craft a well-diversified portfolio tailored to your goals and risk tolerance and how to harness the potential of emerging frontiers like real estate and digital currencies.

But this is just the beginning of your financial exploration. A world of endless possibilities stretches out before you as you stand on the precipice of adulthood, armed with the knowledge and tools you've gained from this book. Your decisions in these pivotal years will lay the foundation for a lifetime of financial security, freedom, and abundance.

Will you take the path of the savvy investor, building a mighty portfolio that will carry you through bull and bear markets? Will you blaze your own trail as a fearless entrepreneur, turning your passions into profitable ventures that change the world? Or will you master the art of side hustling, crafting a life of adventure, flexibility, and ever-growing income streams?

The choice is yours, and the journey ahead will be filled with twists, turns, and unexpected opportunities. But know this: you have what it takes to survive and thrive in the fast-paced, ever-changing landscape of managing your finances in a digital age.

So take a deep breath and embrace the excitement, the uncertainty, and the boundless potential that lies ahead. Trust in the knowledge you've gained, the skills you've honed, and the resilience you've built. The future is yours to shape, and with the power of smart money moving on your side, there's no limit to how high you can soar.

Arnold Bennett wrote in *"How to Live on Twenty-Four Hours a Day"* that *"you can only waste the passing moment. You cannot waste tomorrow; it is kept for you. You cannot waste the next hour; it is kept for you."* This reflects the idea that everyone has the same 24 hours in a day. The key difference between high performers and average individuals is how they use their time.

As you embark on this exhilarating chapter of your financial story, remember the words of the wise Chinese Proverb: ***"The best time to plant a tree was 20 years ago. The second best time is now."*** So plant your seeds of financial wisdom, nurture them with diligence and discipline, and watch in wonder as they grow into a mighty oak of prosperity (a.k.a. the money tree!).

Your financial journey is just beginning, but armed with the knowledge and inspiration from this book, you're ready to take on the world. So, use the tools in this book to make a positive mark on the world and your bank account. The future is yours for the taking.

Remember, this book's knowledge, strategies, and wisdom are only helpful **if you put them into action.** That money tree won't plant itself!

Let's learn and grow together!

Here's to your success!

- Roshel Waite

Sources & References

ABI.org (n.d.) Health Care Costs Number One Cause of Bankruptcy for American Families. American Bankruptcy Institute https://www.abi.org/feed-item/health-care-costs-number-one-cause-of-bankruptcy-for-american-families

Abella, A. (2023 August 31). Robo-Advisors and Young Investors. Investopedia.https://www.investopedia.com/articles/investing/121615/are-roboadvisors-good-idea-young-investors.asp

APA. (2022, March) Stress in America. American Psychological Association. https://www.apa.org/news/press/releases/stress/2022/march-2022-survival-mode

Ascioglu, A., & Maloney, K. (2020). From stock selection to multi-asset investment management. Managerial Finance, 46(5), 647-661.

Abundance Wisdom. (2024, July 23). Retired Billionaire's Sugar Daddy Bank Lesson. Youtube. https://www.youtube.com/shorts/9qDPc_pYo4E

Bennett, A. (2022, April 22). How to Live on Twenty-Four Hours a Day. Double9 Books.

Better Money Habits. (n.d.). How to file your own taxes: 6 steps for beginners. Bank of America. https://bettermoneyhabits.bankofamerica.com/en/taxes-income/how-to-file-your-taxes-in-your-20s

Big Think. (2023, 7th February) Your money trauma starts at childhood. Your Brain on Money. https://www.youtube.com/watch?v=Lu982pPP-_E

Brannon, M. (2023, September 18). Credit Card Debt: 1 in 4 Americans Fall Deeper Into Debt Each Month (2023 Data).

Clever Real Estate Survey. https://listwithclever.com/research/average-american-credit-card-debt-2023/

Brauer, K. (n.d.) New Vs. Used Car Buying: Top 10 Reasons to Buy Used Over New. iSeeCars.com. https://www.iseecars.com/articles/buying-used-vs-new-car

Canada Life (2023, August 15). Four in 10 (41%) UK adults experienced a scam attempt in the last year. https://www.canadalife.co.uk/news/four-in-10-41-uk-adults-experienced-a-scam-attempt-in-the-last-year/

Dweck, C.S. (2006). Mindset: The New Psychology of Success. Random House.

Diekstra, J. (2019). Why you should focus on learning rather than earning to become rich. Medium. https://joey-d.medium.com/why-you-should-focus-on-learning-rather-than-earning-to-become-rich-87718a9dcd7c

Federalreserve.org. (2022). Economic Well-Being of U.S. Households in 2022 - May 2023. https://www.federalreserve.gov/publications/2023-economic-well-being-of-us-households-in-2022-expenses.htm

Fidelity. (n.d.). Guide to diversification. https://www.fidelity.com/viewpoints/investing-ideas/guide-to-diversification

Forbes. (2024, April 12) This Entrepreneur Made $7 Million Investing. Now She's Teaching Other Women How To Do It Too. https://www.youtube.com/watch?v=xLQOyRotOc8

Gillespie, L. (2024 June 20) Bankrate's 2024 Annual Emergency Savings Report. Bankrate. https://www.bankrate.com/banking/savings/emergency-savings-report/

Gov.uk. Check your State Pension age.

https://www.gov.uk/state-pension-age

Greenbook.org (2013, September 22). The Power of Emotional Needs in Consumer Purchases: Insights from Two Studies https://www.greenbook.org/insights/research-methodologies/the-power-of-emotional-needs-in-consumer-purchases-insights-from-two-studies

Greenbook.org (2018, October 8). The Emotional Customer Experience. https://www.greenbook.org/insights/insights/the-emotional-customer-experience

HBR.org. Magid, S., Zorfas. A. et al. (2015). The New Science of Customer Emotions. Harvard Business Review. https://hbr.org/2015/11/the-new-science-of-customer-emotions

Himmelstein, DU, Lawless, R. et al. (2019, March) Medical Bankruptcy: Still Common Despite the Affordable Care Act. https://www.ncbi.nlm.nih.gov/pmc/articles/PMC6366487/ National Library of Medicine (National Center for Biotechnology Information) Am J Public Health. 2019 March; 109(3): 431–433.

Housel, M. (2020). The Psychology of Money. Harriman House.

IdentityTheft.gov. (n.d.). https://www.identitytheft.gov/

Intuit. (2023. January 31). Gen Z Would Rather Talk About Anything But Their Finances. Prosperity Index Study https://www.intuit.com/company/press-room/press-releases/2023/gen-z-would-rather-talk-about-anything-but-their-finances/

Investopedia. (2024 June 19). Cryptocurrency explained with pros and cons for investment. Investopedia. https://www.investopedia.com/terms/c/cryptocurrency.asp

Investopedia. (2024 June 19). A beginner's guide to real estate investing. The Investopedia Team. https://www.investopedia.com/mortgage/real-estate-investing-guide/

Investopedia. (n.d.). Debt Avalanche vs. Debt Snowball: What's the Difference? https://www.investopedia.com/articles/personal-finance/080716/debt-avalanche-vs-debt-snowball-which-best-you.asp

Ipsos (2022l April 22). Over one in three Americans are not considered financially literate. https://www.ipsos.com/en-us/news-polls/money-masters-financial-literacy

IRS. (2022, August 11) College students should study up on these two tax credits. https://www.irs.gov/newsroom/college-students-should-study-up-on-these-two-tax-credits

iseecars.com. (n.d.) New Vs. Used Car Buying: Top 10 Reasons to Buy Used Over New. https://www.iseecars.com/articles/buying-used-vs-new-car

James, T. Modernblkgirl. https://www.modernblkgirl.com/

jobs.ac.uk. (n.d.). Your digital footprint and how to audit it: Career advice. https://career-advice.jobs.ac.uk/jobseeking-and-interview-tips/how-to-audit-your-digital-footprint/

Kiyosaki, R. T. (2017). Rich dad poor dad (2nd ed.). Plata Publishing.

Komase, Y. et al. (2021) Effects of gratitude intervention on Mental Health and well-being among workers: A systematic review, Journal of occupational health. https://www.ncbi.nlm.nih.gov/pmc/articles/PMC8582291/

MyBnk (2023, May 15). Only 2/5 young adults are financially

l i t e r a t e .
https://www.mybnk.org/report-on-financial-education-in-schools/

NerdWallet. (2024). Best High-Yield Online Savings Accounts of March 2024. https://www.nerdwallet.com/best/banking/high-yield-online-savings-accounts

Pchelin, P., & Howell, R. T. (2014). The hidden cost of value-seeking: People do not accurately forecast the economic benefits of experiential purchases. The Journal of Positive Psychology, 9(4), 322–334. https://doi.org/10.1080/17439760.2014.898316

The Ascent. (2021, September 28). Study: The Psychological Cost of Debt. The Motley Fool. https://www.fool.com/the-ascent/research/study-psychological-cost-debt/

Trampe D, Quoidbach J, Taquet M. (2015, Dec) Emotions in Everyday Life. National Library of Medicine https://www.ncbi.nlm.nih.gov/pmc/articles/PMC4689475/

TurboTax. (2024). Tax tip: Filing taxes for freelance workers and self-employed individuals. https://turbotax.intuit.ca/tips/tax-tip-filing-taxes-for-freelance-workers-and-self-employed-individuals-6403

USA.Gov. (n.d.) Learn about your credit report and how to get a copy. Credit Reports. https://www.usa.gov/credit-reports

Warren, E., & Tyagi, A. W. (2005). All your worth: The ultimate lifetime money plan. Simon & Schuster.

Xiao, J. J., & Porto, N. (2019). Present bias and financial behavior. Financial Planning Review, 2(2), e1048.

Tu, V. (2023). *Rich AF: The Money Mindset That Will Change Your Life*. Michael Joseph.

About the author

Roshel Waite is an internet entrepreneur, author, editor, and founder of a popular website (Roshel in a Rush - https://roshelinarush.com/).

Her website provides helpful information & resources on navigating the challenges of Young adulthood & Student life. She helps countless young adults achieve their personal, academic, and professional goals.

To find more of her books, visit her Amazon Author page at:

https://www.amazon.com/author/roshel-waite

Helpful Resources

Do you want a full list of helpful resources to help you level-up your money skills?

BUDGETING TEMPLATES | WORKSHEET | QUIZZES...

- **Roshel in a Rush – website**
  - <https://roshelinarush.com>

- **Resource Library**
  - <https://roshelinarush.com/free-resource-library/>

BUDGETING APPS | TOOLS | SITES...

WEBSITES...

- **Roshel in a Rush – blog**
  - <https://roshelinarush.com/blog>

Scan the QR Code or Click the link to see the FULL list of helpful resources to complement this book.

Made in the USA
Monee, IL
05 January 2025

76124739R00132